POWER
THROUGH CONSTRUCTIVE THINKING

POWER
THROUGH CONSTRUCTIVE
THINKING

EMMET FOX

HarperSanFrancisco

A Division of HarperCollins*Publishers*

FIRST PERENNIAL LIBRARY EDITION PUBLISHED IN 1989

Library of Congress Cataloging-in-Publication Data
Fox, Emmet.
  Power through constructive thinking / Emmet Fox.
    p. cm.
  ISBN 0-06-062861-8
  1. Religion. 2. Prayer. 3. Reincarnation.   I. Title.
BL50.F64   1989   89-45351
291.4′48—dc20   CIP

99 00 01 ❖/RRD H 20 19 18 17

Contents

THE WONDER CHILD   1

THE LORD'S PRAYER   13

THE GOOD SHEPHERD   45

THE SECRET PLACE   51

BE STILL   67

LIGHT AND SALVATION   79

THE EVERLASTING GATES   89

DANIEL IN THE LIONS' DEN   99

THE GARDEN OF ALLAH   107

THE GOLDEN KEY   133

GETTING RESULTS BY PRAYER   137

THE GREAT ADVENTURE   142

YOU MUST BE BORN AGAIN   146

DICK WHITTINGTON   150

THE YOGA OF LOVE   156

YOUR HEART'S DESIRE   163

THE BOGEY MAN UNDER THE STAIRS   172

NO RESULTS WITHOUT PRAYER   176

FAITH   179

THE SEVEN DAY MENTAL DIET   182

LIFE AFTER DEATH   195

REINCARNATION   227

SOWING AND REAPING   257

WHAT IS SCIENTIFIC PRAYER?   259

THE PRESENCE   261

THE WORD OF POWER   263

BLESSING AND CURSING   265

THE GOLDEN GATE   267

TREATMENT FOR DIVINE LOVE   269

GOD IN BUSINESS   270

FIFTEEN POINTS   272

Introduction

THIS book is designed to teach the principles of life building through constructive thought. All power lies in creative thought. Thought is the key to life; for as a man thinketh in his heart, so is he. People are beginning to understand today something of the power of thought to shape the individual's destiny—they know vaguely that thoughts are things—but how the Great Law of thought is to be applied they do not know.

This book shows that your destiny is really in your own hands, because it is impossible to think one thing and produce another, and that by the selection of correct thought a harmonious and happy life is produced. It shows that weak and fickle thinking produces a drifting and wasted life, and that positive thinking produces success and happiness. It shows that fear is the ultimate cause or Tap-Root of all sickness, failure, and disappointment. And it shows the only possible method of overcoming fear.

What you *really* think about any person or any situation is your "treatment" of that condition, and if you wish the condition to change you must know how to "treat" it differently by a change in thought.

But it is also true that the fixed general convictions of your life, as distinct from your current thinking, make you what you are. Your Mental Conduct, your hour-by-hour thinking, produces specific conditions, and may be thought of as the weather of your soul. Your fixed convictions concerning the things that really matter are seldom changed and may be called the climate of the soul, and it is these that mold your destiny.

What do you really believe about the great problems of life? What do you think about your relationship to God? What sort of God do you worship? Do you think that prayer really makes any difference? Are you merely praying to a magnified edition of yourself; or are you worshipping the true God in spirit and in truth? What do you think about life after death? Do you think that you have ever lived before? Are you nourishing a grievance at the bottom of your heart because you think you were born into unfavorable conditions?

Why is one man sick and another man well? Why does one man live in a happy, comfortable home and another drag out a meager existence in a slum? Why is one man popular and respected and another man disliked, or at least ignored? Why does one man produce a great work while another falters through life without ever doing anything worth while? Why are so many sincerely religious people unhappy and frustrated? Why are many earnest Bible students unable to solve a single one of their own problems? Why is it that learned men and philosophers are notoriously unsuccessful in the business of personal living, if it is really true that "knowledge is power"?

It is necessary for you to realize that it is your considered attitude to such questions as these that ultimately determines everything in your life from the state of your body to the daily work that you do and the kind of people that you meet.

This book is intended to help people to clarify their thinking on these important points. It is an attempt to explain the fundamental Truth of Being in the simple language of everyday life. The author has always believed that it must be possible to explain the most profound truths of religion and philosophy in the simplest language; and he has made it a rule both in his writings and on the platform never to employ any word that is not in common use in offices, workshops, street cars, and so forth.

Some knowledge of metaphysics or spiritual truth is absolutely essential if you are to understand yourself and to take over effectual control of your life, and this book deals with the subject from several different angles.

The teaching in this book is founded on the Bible. The Bible is not like any other book; it is a spiritual vortex through which spiritual power pours from heaven to earth, and the reason why most people derive comparatively little profit from its study is that they lack the spiritual key.

You can have power to make your life healthy, happy, useful, and outstandingly successful, if you will study the laws of life, and apply them faithfully.

All the essays in this book have previously been published as separate pamphlets and are still obtainable in that form. This collected edition is put out in response to very many requests from all over the world.

The Wonder Child

S TRANGE as it may seem to you, there exists a mystic power that is able to transform your life so thoroughly, so radically, so completely, that when the process is completed your own friends would hardly recognize you, and, in fact, you would scarcely be able to recognize yourself. You would sit down and ask yourself: "Can I really be the man or woman that I vaguely remember, who went about under my name six months or six years ago? Was I really that person? Could that person possibly have been I?" And the truth will be that while in one sense you are indeed the same person, yet in another sense you will be someone utterly different. This mystic but intensely real force can pick you up today, *now*, from the midst of failure, ruin, misery, despair—and in the twinkling of an eye, as Paul said, solve your problems, smooth out your difficulties, cut you free from any entanglements, and place you clear, safe, and happy upon the highroad of freedom and opportunity.

It can lift you out of an invalid's bed, make you sound and well once more, and free to go out into the world to shape your life as you will. It can throw open the prison door and liberate the captive. It has a magical healing balm for the bruised or broken heart.

This mystic Power can teach you all things that you need to know, if only you are receptive and teachable.

1

It can inspire you with new thoughts and ideas, so that your work may be truly original. It can impart new and wonderful kinds of knowledge as soon as you really want such knowledge—glorious knowledge—strange things not taught in schools or written in books. It can do for you that which is probably the most important thing of all in your present stage: it can find your true place in life for you, and put you into it too. It can find the right friends for you, kindred spirits who are interested in the same ideas and want the same things that you do. It can provide you with an ideal home. It can furnish you with the prosperity that means freedom, freedom to be and to do and to go as your soul calls.

This extraordinary Power, mystic though I have rightly called it, is nevertheless very real, no mere imaginary abstraction, but actually the most practical thing there is. The existence of this Power is already well known to thousands of people in the world today, and has been known to certain enlightened souls for tens of thousands of years. This Power is really no less than the primal Power of Being, and to discover that Power is the Divine birthright of all men. It is your right and your privilege to make your contact with this Power, and to allow it to work through your body, mind, and estate, so that you need no longer grovel upon the ground amid limitations and difficulties, but can soar up on wings like an eagle to the realm of dominion and joy.

But where, it will naturally be asked, is the wonderful, mystic Power to be contacted? Where may we find it? and how is it brought into action? The answer is perfectly simple—This Power is to be found within your own consciousness, the last place that most people would loook for it. Right within your own mentality there lies a source of energy stronger than electricity, more potent than high explosive; unlimited and inexhaustible. You only need to make conscious contact with this Power to set it working in your affairs; and all the marvelous results enumerated can be yours. This is the real meaning of such sayings in the Bible as "The Kingdom of God is within you"; and "Seek ye first the Kingdom of God, and all the rest shall be added."

This Indwelling Power, the Inner Light, or Spiritual Idea, is spoken of in the Bible as a child, and throughout the Scriptures the child symbolically always stands for this. Bible symbolism has its own beautiful logic, and just as the soul is always spoken of as a woman, so this, the Spiritual Idea that is born to the soul, is described as a child. The conscious discovery by you that you have this Power within you, and your determination to make use of it, is the birth of the child. And it is easy to see how very apt the symbol is, for the infant that is born in consciousness is just such a weak, feeble entity as any new-born child, and it calls for the same careful nursing and guarding that any infant does in its earliest days. After a time, however, as the weeks go by, the child grows stronger and bigger, until a time comes when it can well take care of itself; and then it grows and grows in wisdom and stature until, no longer leaning on the mother's care, the child, now arrived at man's estate, turns the tables, and repays its debt by taking over the care of its mother. So your ability to contact the mystic Power within yourself, frail and feeble at first, will gradually develop until you find yourself permitting that Power to take your whole life into its care.

The life story of Jesus, the central figure of the Bible, perfectly dramatizes this truth. He is described as being born of a virgin, and in a poor stable, and we know how he grew up to be the Saviour of the world. Now, in Bible symbolism, the virgin soul means the soul that looks to God alone, and it is this condition of soul in which the child, or Spiritual Idea, comes to birth. It is when we have reached that stage, the stage where, either through wisdom or because of suffering, we are prepared to put God really first, that the thing happens.

The Christ Child was born in a stable, though all the world had anticipated that when He arrived it would be in a palace; and we deeply appreciate the significance of this point as soon as the Holy Child comes to birth in our own soul, for with the natural consciousness of our own unworthiness we feel only too keenly that once more He is indeed being born in a stable. Here we have the inspired intimation that this fact will not prevent His growing up to be the saviour of our own individual world.

The Bible directly and indirectly has a good deal to say on the subject of the birth and growth of the child, and what it can mean for us. One of the most significant pronouncements on this subject is given in the Book of Isaiah, Chapter 9, verses 2, 6, and 7, and it will amply repay us to consider that statement in some detail.

Isaiah says: "The peoople that walked in darkness have seen a great light: they that dwell in the land of the shadow of death, upon them hath the light shined." This is a marvelous description of what happens when the Spiritual Idea, the child, is born to the soul. Walking in darkness, moral or physical, dwelling in the land of the shadow of death—the death of joy, or hope, or even self-respect—describes well the condition of many people before this light shines into their weary, heartbroken lives; and the Prophet rises into a paean of exultant joy as he contemplates the deliverance wrought by the mystic Power: "For unto us a child is born, unto us a son is given: and the government shall be upon his shoulder: and his name shall be called Wonderful, Counsellor, The Mighty God, The Everlasting Father, The Prince of Peace."

This description begins by giving the gist of the whole matter, simply and concisely—that the government is to be upon *his* shoulder. This really covers the whole business. Correctly understood, this statement tells the entire story without need of any further comment. It means that once you have contacted the mystic Power within, and have allowed it to take over your responsibilities for you, it will direct and govern all your affairs from the greatest to the least without effort, and without mistakes, and without trouble to you. *The government shall be upon his shoulder.* You are tired, and driven, and worried, and weak, and ill, and depressed, because you have been trying to carry the government upon your own shoulder; the burden is too much for you, and you have broken down under it. Now, immediately you hand over your self-government, that is, the burden of making a living, or of healing your body, or erasing your mistakes, to the Child, He, the Tireless One, the All-Powerful, the All-Wise, the All-Resourceful, assumes it with joy; and your difficulties have seen the beginning of the end.

The Prophet next goes on to speak of the "Name" of the child, and if we know something of Bible symbolism, we know that we are now going to learn something fundamental, for in the Bible, the *name* of anything, means the character or nature of that thing, and so we realize that a name is not merely an arbitrary label, but actually a hieroglyph of the soul. We are given no less than five names or qualities of the child. Let us examine them and see what they tell us. First of all, Isaiah says that the name of the child is Wonderful, and this in fact is the first and the outstanding quality; this child is a Wonder Child. The word "wonderful" used here requires to be carefully scrutinized. As employed in the Bible, it implies simply and plainly a miracle—a miracle, just that, and nothing less, because you have to realize that the Bible teaches the miracle from the first page to the last. The Bible repeatedly says that miracles can happen, and that they do happen; and it gives detailed and circumstantial accounts of many specific cases. And it says, many times, that miracles always will happen if you believe them to be possible, and are willing to recognize the Power of God, and to call upon it.

There have been many efforts during the last two generations to divorce the Bible teaching from the belief in miracles. Attempts have been made to show that in some unexplained way the Bible can be true and useful, and yet mistaken in its teaching of the miracle; in other words, that it can in some mysterious manner be an edifying conglomeration of truth and lies. Indeed, one famous Bible critic said blandly: "Miracles do not happen"—thus dismissing the whole matter with a wave of his hand. The obvious rejoinder to this is that if it were true that miracles do not happen, the Bible would be a mere meaningless jumble of pointless fables. But they do happen, and even as Galileo terminated the other controversy by saying, "nevertheless it revolves," so when all controversy finishes, we may say of miracles "nevertheless, they happen."

Well now, just recollect the first quality that Isaiah gives for the child. It is a *wonder* child; that is to say, it is a miraculous child; it is a worker of miracles. This means that as soon as the Wonder Child is born in your consciousness, the miracle will come into your life—a real miracle, remember. This does not mean simply that you will become resigned to your present circumstances, or merely that you will then be enabled to meet the same difficulties with a higher courage or a clearer brain. It means the *miracle*. It means that the Wonder Child, not in any figurative or metaphorical sense, but plainly and literally, in the most matter of fact meaning of the term, will work miracles in your life. It will do these things absolutely, irrespective of what your present conditions are. It is in no way constrained or constricted by your present circumstances. The whole point is that the Wonder Child can lift you out of those very circumstances, and set you down in different circumstances. The Wonder Child is the Miracle Child.

Now let us take the second point that the Prophet gives us concerning this Wonder Child. He calls it "Counsellor," and a counsellor, you know, is one who gives advice or guidance; and so you see that once the Child has been born, you need never again lack either of these things. The Child will be your infallible counsellor. If you are worried because you do not know whether or not to take some important step, to accept or reject a business offer, to sign or not to sign an important document, to enter upon or to dissolve a partnership, to resign your position or not, to go abroad or to stay at home, to trust someone or not to trust him, to say something or to leave it unsaid, the Wonder Child will be your Counsellor, and the Wonder Child is never mistaken.

It is in the third point that the Prophet reveals to us who the Wonder Child really is. It is no less than God Himself, "The Mighty God," as Isaiah reminds us, and truly the mystic Power that transforms, and transmutes, and transfigures, is *God Himself,* always present with you, and always available, once you have understood and accepted the Spiritual Idea. And it is because He is God, that the work of the Child is independent of all conditions.

The fourth name that the Prophet attributes to the Child is that of Everlasting Father. This point establishes our relationship to God in unmistakable terms. As Jesus so clearly pointed out, God is our Father, not merely our Creator, and we as the children of a good Father may expect to find ourselves provided with everything that we need for body or soul. But since we have to establish for ourselves our own consciousness of this fact, and as our demonstration is just the measure of our understanding of it, our concept of the Divine fact is the fruit of our own soul, and may mystically be called our child.

Finally, in the fifth point, we receive what is perhaps the greatest name of all. Here the Child is called "The Prince of Peace." Just try to realize a little what this title must mean for you in practice—nothing less than that the Wonder Child, the Spiritual Idea, born to your own soul, is the Prince of Peace. Now think what perfect peace of soul, if you could attain it, would actually mean to you. If your soul were truly at peace, what in your life could go wrong? If only you had real peace of soul, do you suppose that your body could be ill? Given real peace of soul, how easy it would be to find your true place in the world, which would mean prosperity as well as happiness. How easily, how quickly and efficiently you could perform your work, work such as you have never done yet, and in less than half the usual time. Of course, everybody knows that this is what would follow the attainment of soul peace, but there is still much more in it than that. What you perhaps do not know is that once you have attained true peace of soul, you have made it possible for the Mystic Power, the Wonder Child, to teach you new things, utterly beyond the compass of your present understanding, enabling you to do things in the world, if you should wish to, that nobody would have deemed it possible that you could do. Well, it is in the very nature of the Wonder Child to give you just that very soul peace, and it is because of this function that it is called "The Prince of Peace."

Isaiah goes on to tell us that this is no limited demonstration, but that once it begins, it goes on and on as we rise higher and higher in consciousness, increasing and expanding more and more unto the perfect day. "Of the increase of his government and peace there shall be no end, upon the throne of David, and upon his kingdom, to order it, and to establish it with judgment and with justice from henceforth even forever." The throne of David is of course Jerusalem, which is Uru-Salem, the city of peace, this very peace that we have been discussing; and Jerusalem symbolically is the awakened consciousness. There shall indeed be no end to the increase of *that* government, and in view of the possibility that the weaker souls, the fearful, and the unbelieving, and the depressed, should find it impossible to believe that such good things could possibly be true, the Prophet clinches the matter with the definite assertion: "The Zeal of the Lord of Hosts will perform this." This should remove all sense of personal responsibility for the demonstration, the bugbear of so many seekers. Have we not seen that the gist of the whole matter is just this very point—that the government shall be upon *his* shoulder.

Our Father, which art in heaven, Hallowed be thy name. Thy kingdom come. Thy will be done, in earth as it is in heaven. Give us this day our daily bread. And forgive us our trespasses, as we forgive them that trespass against us. And lead us not into temptation; but deliver us from evil: For thine is the kingdom, the power, and the glory, for ever and ever.

Amen.

The Lord's Prayer

T HE Lord's Prayer is the most important of all the Christian documents. It was carefully constructed by Jesus with certain very clear ends in view. That is why, of all his teachings, it is by far the best known, and the most often quoted. It is, indeed, the one common denominator of all the Christian churches. Every one of them, without exception, uses the Lord's Prayer; it is perhaps the only ground upon which they all meet. Every Christian child is taught the Lord's Prayer, and any Christian who prays at all says it almost every day. Its actual use probably exceeds that of all other prayers put together. Undoubtedly everyone who is seeking to follow along the Way that Jesus led, should make a point of using the Lord's Prayer, and using it intelligently, every day.

In order to do this, we should understand that the Prayer is a carefully constructed organic whole. Many people rattle through it like parrots, forgetful of the warning that Jesus gave us against vain repetitions, and, of course, no one derives any profit from that sort of thing.

The Great Prayer is a compact formula for the development of the soul. It is designed with the utmost care for that specific purpose; so that those who use it regularly, with understanding, will experience a real change of soul. The only progress is this change, which is what the Bible calls being born again. It is the change of soul that matters. The mere acquisition of fresh knowledge received intellectually makes no change in the soul. The Lord's Prayer is especially designed to bring this change about, and when it is regularly used it invariably does so.

The more one analyzes the Lord's Prayer, the more wonderful is its construction seen to be. It meets everyone's need just at his own level. It not only provides a rapid spiritual development for those who are sufficiently advanced to be ready, but in its superficial meaning it supplies the more simple-minded and even the more materially minded people with just what they need at the moment, if they use the Prayer sincerely.

This greatest of all prayers was designed with still another purpose in view, quite as important as either of the others. Jesus foresaw that, as the centuries went by, his simple, primitive teaching would gradually become overlain by all sorts of external things which really have nothing whatever to do with it. He foresaw that men who had never known him, relying, quite sincerely, no doubt, upon their own limited intellects, would build up theologies and doctrinal systems, obscuring the direct simplicity of the spiritual message, and actually erecting a wall between God and man. He designed his Prayer in such a way that it would pass safely through those ages without being tampered with. He arranged it with consummate skill, so that it could not be twisted or distorted, or adapted to any man-made system; so that, in fact, it would carry the whole Christ Message within it, and yet not have anything on the surface to attract the attention to the restless, managing type of person. So it has turned out that through all the changes and chances of Christian history, this Prayer has come through to us uncorrupted and unspoiled.

The first thing that we notice is that the Prayer naturally falls into seven clauses. This is very characteristic of the Oriental tradition. Seven symbolizes individual completeness, the perfection of the individual soul, just as the number twelve in the same convention stands for corporate completeness. In practical use, we often find an eighth clause added—"Thine is the kingdom, the power, and the glory"—but this, though in itself an excellent affirmation, is not really a part of the Prayer. The seven clauses are put together with the utmost care, in perfect order and sequence, and they contain everything that is necessary for the nourishment of the soul. Let us consider the first clause:

Our Father

This simple statement in itself constitutes a definite and complete system of theology. It fixes clearly and distinctly the nature and character of God. It sums up the Truth of Being. It tells all that man needs to know about God, and about himself, and about his neighbor. Anything that is added to this can only be by way of commentary, and is more likely than not to complicate and obscure the true meaning of the text. Oliver Wendell Holmes said: "My religion is summed up in the first two words of the Lord's Prayer," and most of us will find ourselves in full agreement with him.

Notice the simple, clear-cut, definite statement—"Our Father." In this clause Jesus lays down once and for all that the relationship between God and man is that of father and child. This cuts out any possibility that the Deity could be the relentless and cruel tyrant that is often pictured by theology. Jesus says definitely that the relationship is that of parent and child; not an Oriental despot dealing with grovelling slaves, but parent and child. Now we all know perfectly well that men and women, however short they may fall in other respects, nearly always do the best they can for their children. Unfortunately, cruel and wicked parents are to be found, but they are so exceptional as to make a paragraph for the newspapers. The vast majority of men and women are at their best in dealing with their children. Speaking of the same truth elsewhere, Jesus said: "If you, who are so full of evil, nevertheless do your best for your children, how much more will God, who is altogether good, do for you"; and so he begins his Prayer by establishing the character of God as that of the perfect Father dealing with His children.

Note that this clause which fixes the nature of God, at the same time fixes the nature of man, because if man is the offspring of God, he must partake of the nature of God, since the nature of the offspring is invariably similar to that of the parent. It is a Cosmic Law that like begets like. It is not possible that a rosebush should produce lilies, or that a cow should give birth to a colt. The offspring is and must be of the same nature as the parent; and so, since God is Divine Spirit, man must essentially be Divine Spirit too, whatever appearances may say to the contrary.

Let us pause here for a moment and try to realize what a tremendous step forward we have taken in appreciating the teaching of Jesus on this point. Do you not see that at a single blow it swept away ninety-nine per cent of all the old theology, with its avenging God, its chosen and favored individuals, its eternal hell fire, and all the other horrible paraphernalia of man's diseased and terrified imagination. God exists—and the Eternal, All-Powerful, All-Present God is the loving Father of mankind.

If you would meditate upon this fact, until you had some degree of understanding of what it really means, most of your difficulties and physical ailments would disappear, for they are rooted and grounded in fear. The underlying cause of *all* trouble is fear. If only you could realize to some extent that Omnipotent Wisdom is your living, loving Father, most of your fears would go. If you could realize it completely, every negative thing in your life would vanish away, and you would demonstrate perfection in every phase. Now you see the object that Jesus had in mind when he placed this clause first.

Next we see that the Prayer says, not "My Father," but "Our Father," and this indicates, beyond the possibility of mistake, the truth of the brotherhood of man. It forces upon our attention at the very beginning the fact that all men are indeed brethren, the children of one Father; and that "there is neither Jew nor Greek, there is neither bond nor free, there is neither chosen nor unchosen," because all men are brethren. Here Jesus in making his second point, ends all the tiresome nonsense about a "chosen race," about the spiritual superiority of any one group of human beings over any other group. He cuts away the illusion that the members of any nation, or race, or territory, or group, or class, or color, are, in the sight of God, superior to any other group. A belief in the superiority of one's own particular group, or "herd," as the psychologists call it, is an illusion to which mankind is very prone, but in the teaching of Jesus it has no place. He teaches that the thing that places a man is the spiritual condition of his own individual soul, and that as long as he is upon the spiritual path it makes no difference whatever to what group he belongs or does not belong.

The final point is the implied command that we are to pray not only for ourselves but for all mankind. Every student of Truth should hold the thought of the Truth of Being for the whole human race for at least a moment each day, since none of us lives to himself nor dies to himself; for indeed we are all truly—and in a much more literal sense than people are aware—limbs of one Body.

Now we begin to see how very much more than appears on the surface is contained in those simple words "Our Father." Simple—one might almost say innocent—as they look, Jesus has concealed within them a spiritual explosive that will ultimately destroy every man-made system that holds the human race in bondage.

Which art in heaven

Having clearly established the Fatherhood of God and the brotherhood of man, Jesus next goes on to enlarge upon the nature of God, and to describe the fundamental facts of existence. Having shown that God and man are parent and child, he goes on to delineate the function of each in the grand scheme of things. He explains that it is the nature of God to be in heaven, and of man to be on earth, because God is Cause, and man is manifestation. Cause cannot be expression, and expression cannot be cause, and we must be careful not to confuse the two things. Here heaven stands for God or Cause, because in religious phraseology heaven is the term for the Presence of God. In metaphysics it is called the Absolute, because it is the realm of Pure Unconditioned Being, or archetypal ideas. The word "earth" means manifestation, and man's function is to manifest or express God, or Cause. In other words, God is the Infinite and Perfect Cause of all things; but Cause has to be expressed, and God expresses Himself by means of man. Man's destiny is to express God in all sorts of glorious and wonderful ways. Some of this expression we see as his surroundings; first his physical body, which is really only the most intimate part of his embodiment; then his home; his work; his recreation; in short, his whole expression. To express means to press outward, or bring into sight that which already exists implicitly. Every feature of your life is really a manifestation or expression of something in your soul.

Some of these points may seem at first to be a little abstract; but since it is misunderstandings about the relationship of God and man that lead to all our difficulties, it is worth any amount of trouble correctly to understand that relationship. Trying to have manifestation without Cause, is atheism and materialism, and we know where they lead. Trying to have Cause without manifestation leads man to suppose himself to be a personal God, and this commonly ends in megalomania and a kind of paralysis of expression.

The important thing to realize is that God is in heaven and man on earth, and that each has his own role in the scheme of things. Although they are One, they are not one-and-the-same. Jesus establishes this point carefully when he says, "Our Father which art in heaven."

Hallowed be thy name

In the Bible, as elsewhere, the "name" of anything means the essential nature or character of that thing, and so, when we are told what the name of God is, we are told what His nature is, and His name or nature, Jesus says, is "hallowed." Now what does the word "hallowed" mean? Well, if you trace the derivation back into Old English, you will discover a most extraordinarily interesting and significant fact. The word "hallowed" has the same meaning as "holy," "whole," "wholesome," "heal," or "healed"; so we see that the nature of God is not merely worthy of our veneration, but is complete and perfect—altogether good. Some very remarkable consequences follow from this. We have agreed that an effect must be similar in its nature to its cause, and so, because the nature of God is hallowed, everything that follows from that Cause must be hallowed or perfect too. Just as a rose-bush cannot produce lilies, so God cannot cause or send anything but perfect good. As the Bible says, "the same fountain cannot send forth both sweet and bitter water." From this it follows that God cannot, as people sometimes think, send sickness or trouble, or accidents—much less death—for these things are unlike His nature. "Hallowed be thy name" means "Thy nature is altogether good, and Thou art the author only of perfect good." *Of purer eyes than to behold evil, and canst not look on iniquity.*

If you think that God has sent any of your difficulties to you, for no matter how good a reason, you are giving power to your troubles, and this makes it very difficult to get rid of them.

Thy kingdom come. Thy will be done, in earth as it is in heaven

Man being *man*ifestation or expression of God has a limitless destiny before him. His work is to express, in concrete, definite form, the abstract ideas with which God furnishes him, and in order to do this, he must have creative power. If he did not have creative power, he would be merely a machine through which God worked—an automaton. But man is not automaton; he is an individualized consciousness. God individualizes Himself in an infinite number of distinct focal points of consciousness, each one quite different; and therefore each one is a distinct way of knowing the universe, each a distinct experience. Notice carefully that the word "individual" means *undivided*. The consciousness of each one is distinct from God and from all others, and yet none are separated. How can this be? How can two things be one, and yet not one and the same? The answer is that in matter, which is finite, they cannot; but in Spirit, which is infinite, they can. With our present limited, three-dimensional consciousness, we cannot see this; but intuitively we can understand it through prayer. If God did not individualize Himself, there would be only one experience; as it is, there are as many universes as there are individuals to form them through thinking.

"Thy kingdom come" means that it is our duty to be ever occupied in helping to establish the Kingdom of God on earth. That is to say, our work is to bring more and more of God's ideas into concrete manifestation upon this plane. That is what we are here for. The old saying, "God has a plan for every man, and he has one for you," is quite correct. God has glorious and wonderful plans for every one of us; he has planned a splendid career, full of interest, life, and joy, for each, and if our lives are dull, or restricted, or squalid, that is not His fault, but ours.

If only you will find out the thing God intends you do to, and will do it, you will find that all doors will open to you; all obstacles in your path will melt away; you will be acclaimed a brilliant success; you will be most liberally rewarded from the monetary point of view; and you will be gloriously happy.

There is a true place in life for each one of us, upon the attainment of which we shall be completely happy, and perfectly secure. On the other hand, until we do find our true place we never shall be either happy or secure, no matter what other things we may have. Our true place is the one place where we can bring the Kingdom of God into manifestation, and truly say, "Thy kingdom cometh."

We have seen that man too often chooses to use his free will in a negative way. He allows himself to think wrongly, selfishly, and this wrong thinking brings upon him all his troubles. Instead of understanding that it is his essential nature to express God, to be ever about his Father's business, he tries to set up upon his own account. All our troubles arise from just this folly. We abuse our free will, trying to work apart from God; and the very natural result is all the sickness, poverty, sin, trouble, and death that we find on the physical plane. We must never for a moment try to live for ourselves, or make plans or arrangements without reference to God, or suppose that we can be either happy or successful if we are seeking any other end than to do His Will. Whatever our desire may be, whether it be something concerning our daily work, or our duty at home, our relations with our fellow man, or private plans for the employment of our own time, if we seek to serve self instead of God, we are ordering trouble, disappointment, and unhappiness, notwithstanding what the evidence to the contrary may seem to be. Whereas, if we choose what, through prayer, we know to be His Will, then we are insuring for ourselves ultimate success, freedom, and joy, however much self-sacrifice and self-discipline it may involve at the moment.

Our business is to bring our whole nature as fast as we can into conformity with the Will of God, by constant prayer and unceasing, though unanxious, watching. "Our wills are ours to make them Thine."
"In His Will is our peace," said Dante, and the Divine Comedy is really a study in fundamental states of consciousness, the Inferno representing the state of the soul that is endeavoring to live without God, the Paradiso representing the state of the soul that has achieved its conscious unity with the Divine Will, and the Purgatorio the condition of the soul that is struggling to pass from the one state to the other. It was this sublime conflict of the soul which wrung from the heart of the great Augustine the cry, "Thou has made us for Thyself, and our hearts are restless until they repose in Thee."

Give us this day our daily bread

Because we are the children of a loving Father, we are entitled to expect that God will provide us fully with everything we need. Children naturally and spontaneously look to their human parents to supply all their wants, and in the same way we should look to God to supply ours. If we do so, in faith and understanding, we shall never look in vain.

It is the Will of God that we should all lead healthy, happy lives, full of joyous experience; that we should develop freely and steadily, day by day and week by week, as our pathways unfold more and more unto the perfect day. To this end we require such things as food, clothing, shelter, means of travel, books, and so on; above all, we require *freedom;* and in the Prayer all these things are included under the heading of bread. Bread, that is to say, means not merely food in general, but all things that man requires for a healthy, happy, free, and harmonious life. But in order to obtain these things, we have to claim them, not necessarily in detail, but *we have to claim them,* and, we have to recognize God and God alone as the Source and fountainhead of all our good. Lack of any kind is always traceable to the fact that we have been seeking our supply from some secondary source, instead of from God, Himself, the Author and Giver of life.

People think of their supply as coming from certain investments, or from a business, or from an employer, perhaps; whereas these are merely the channels through which it comes, God being the Source. The number of possible channels is infinite, the Source is One. The particular channel through which you are getting your supply is quite likely to change, because change is the Cosmic Law for manifestation. Stagnation is really death; but as long as you realize that the *Source* of your supply is the one unchangeable Spirit, all is well. The fading out of one channel will be but the signal for the opening of another. If, on the other hand, like most people, you regard the particular channel as being the source, then when that channel fails, as it is very likely to do, you are left stranded, because you *believe* that the source has dried up—and for practical purposes, on the physical plane, things are as we believe them to be.

A man, for instance, thinks of his employment as the source of his income, and for some reason he loses it. His employer goes out of business, or cuts down the staff, or they have a falling out. Now, because he believes that his position is the source of his income, the loss of the position naturally means the loss of the income, and so he has to start looking about for another job, and perhaps has to look a long time, meanwhile finding himself without apparent supply. If such a man had realized, through regular daily Treatment, that God was his supply, and his job only the particular channel through which it came, then upon the closing of that channel, he would have found another, and probably a better one, opening immediately. If his belief had been in God as his supply, then since God cannot change or fail, or fade out, his supply would have come from *somewhere,* and would have formed its own channel in whatever was the easiest way.

In precisely the same way the proprietor of a business may find himself obliged to close down for some cause outside of his control; or one whose income is dependent upon stocks or bonds may suddenly find that source dried up, owing to unexpected happenings on the stock market, or to some catastrophe to a factory or a mine. If he regards the business or the investment as his *source* of supply, he will believe his source to have collapsed, and will in consequence be left stranded; whereas, if his reliance is upon God, he will be comparatively indifferent to the channel and so that channel will be easily supplanted by a new one. In short, we have to train ourselves to look to God, Cause, for all that we need, and then the channel, which is entirely a secondary matter, will take care of itself.

In its inner and most important meaning, our daily bread signifies the realization of the Presence of God—an actual sense that God exists not merely in a nominal way, but as *the* great reality; the sense that He is present with us; and the feeling that because He is God, all good, all powerful, all wise, and all loving, we have nothing to fear; that we can rely upon Him to take every care of us; that He will supply all that we need to have; teach us all that we need to know; and guide our steps so that we shall not make mistakes. This is Emanuel, or God with us; and remember that it absolutely means some degree of actual *realization*, that is to say, some experience in consciousness, and not just a theoretical recognition of the fact; not simply talking about God, however beautifully one may talk, or *thinking about* Him; but some degree of actual experience. We must begin by thinking about God, but this should lead to the realization which is the *daily bread* or manna. That is the gist of the whole matter. Realization, which is experience, is the thing that counts. It is realization which marks the progress of the soul. It is realization which guarantees the demonstration. It is realization, as distinct from mere theorizing and fine words, which is the *substance of things hoped for, the evidence of things not seen.* This is the Bread of Life, the hidden manna, and when one has that, he has all things in deed and in truth. Jesus several times refers to this experience as bread because it is the nourishment of the soul, just as physical food is the nourishment of the physical body. Supplied with this food, the soul grows and waxes strong, gradually developing to adult stature. Without it, she, being deprived of her essential nourishment, is naturally stunted and crippled.

The common mistake, of course, is to suppose that a formal recognition of God is sufficient, or that talking about Divine things, perhaps talking very poetically, is the same as possessing them; but this is exactly on a par with supposing that looking at a tray of food, or discussing the chemical composition of sundry foodstuffs, is the same thing as actually eating a meal. It is this mistake which is responsible for the fact that people sometimes pray for a thing for years without any tangible result. If prayer is a force at all, it cannot be possible to pray without something happening.

A realization cannot be obtained to order; it must come spontaneously as the result of regular daily prayer. To seek realization by will power is the surest way to miss it. Pray regularly and quietly—remember that in all mental work, *effort* or strain defeats itself—then presently, perhaps when you least expect it, like a thief in the night, the realization will come. Meanwhile it is well to know that all sorts of practical difficulties can be overcome by sincere prayer, without any realization at all. Good workers have said that they have had some of their best demonstrations without any realization worth speaking about; but while it is, of course, a wonderful boon to surmount such particular difficulties, we do not achieve the sense of security and well-being to which we are entitled until we have experienced realization.

Another reason why the food or bread symbol for the experience of the Presence of God is such a telling one, is that the act of eating food is essentially a thing that must be done for oneself. No one can assimilate food for another. One may hire servants to do all sorts of other things for him; but there is one thing that one must positively do for himself, and that is to eat his own food. In the same way, the realization of the Presence of God is a thing that no one else can have for us. We can and should help one another in the overcoming of specific difficulties—"Bear ye one another's burdens"—but the realization (or making real) of the Presence of God, the "substance" and "evidence," can, in the nature of things, be had only at first hand.

In speaking of the "bread of life, Emanuel," Jesus calls it our *daily* bread. The reason for this is very fundamental—our contact with God must be a living one. It is our *momentary* attitude to God which governs our being. "Behold *now* is the day of salvation." The most futile thing in the world is to seek to live upon a past realization. The thing that means spiritual life to you is your realization of God *here and now.*

Today's realization, no matter how feeble and poor it may seem, has a million times more power to help you than the most vivid realization of yesterday. Be thankful for yesterday's experience, knowing that it is with you forever in the change of consciousness which it brought about, but do not lean upon it for a single moment for the need of today. Divine Spirit *is,* and changes not with the ebb and flow of human apprehension. The manna in the desert is the Old Testament prototype of this. The people wandering in the wilderness were told that they would be supplied with manna from heaven every day, each one always receiving abundant for his needs, but they were on no account to try to save it up for the morrow. They were on no account to endeavor to live upon yesterday's food, and when, notwithstanding the rule, some of them did try to do so, the result was pestilence or death.

So it is with us. When we seek to live upon yesterday's realization, we are actually seeking to live in the past, and to live in the past is death. The art of life is to live in the present moment, and to make that moment as perfect as we can by the realization that we are the instruments and expression of God Himself. The best way to prepare for tomorrow is to make today all that it should be.

Forgive us our trespasses, as we forgive them that trespass against us

This clause is the turning point of the Prayer. It is the strategic key to the whole Treatment. Let us notice here that Jesus has so arranged this marvelous Prayer that it covers the entire ground of the unfoldment of our souls completely, and in the most concise and telling way. It omits nothing that is essential for our salvation, and yet, so compact is it that there is not a thought or a word too much. Every idea fits into its place with perfect harmony and in perfect sequence. Anything more would be redundance, anything less would be incompleteness, and at this point it takes up the critical factor of forgiveness.

Having told us what God is, what man is, how the universe works, how we are to do our own work—the salvation of humanity and of our own souls—he then explains what our true nourishment or supply is, and the way in which we can obtain it; and now he comes to the forgiveness of sins.

The forgiveness of sins is the central problem of life. Sin is a sense of separation from God, and is the major tragedy of human experience. It is, of course, rooted in selfishness. It is essentially an attempt to gain some supposed good to which we are not entitled in justice. It is a sense of isolated, self-regarding, personal existence, whereas the Truth of being is that all is One. Our true selves are at one with God, undivided from

Him, expressing His ideas, witnessing to His nature—
the dynamic Thinking of that Mind. Because we are
all one with the great Whole of which we are spiritually a part, it follows that we are one with all men. Just
because in Him we live and move and have our being,
we are, in the absolute sense, all essentially one.

Evil, sin, the fall of man, in fact, is essentially the
attempt to negate this Truth in our thoughts. We try
to live apart from God. We try to do without Him. We
act as though we had life of our own; as separate
minds; as though we could have plans and purposes
and interests separate from His. All this, if it were true,
would mean that existence is not one and harmonious,
but a chaos of competition and strife. It would mean
that we are quite separate from our fellow man and
could injure him, rob him, or hurt him, or even destroy him, without any damage to ourselves, and, in
fact, that the more we took from other people the
more we should have for ourselves. It would mean
that the more we considered our own interests, and
the more indifferent we were to the welfare of others,
the better off we should be. Of course it would then
follow naturally that it would pay others to treat us in
the same way, and that accordingly we might expect
many of them to do so. Now if this were true, it would
mean that the whole universe is only a jungle, and that
sooner or later it must destroy itself by its own inherent weakness and anarchy. But, of course, it is not
true, and therein lies the joy of life.

Undoubtedly, many people do act as though they
believed it to be true, and a great many more, who
would be dreadfully shocked if brought face to face
with that proposition in cold blood, have, nevertheless, a vague feeling that such must be very much the

way things are, even though they, themselves, are personally above consciously acting in accordance with such a notion. Now this is the real basis of sin, of resentment, of condemnation, of jealousy, of remorse, and all the evil brood that walk that path.

This belief in independent and separate existence is the arch sin, and now, before we can progress any further, we have to take the knife to this evil thing and cut it out once and for all. Jesus knew this, and with this definite end in view he inserted at this critical point a carefully prepared statement that would compass our end and his, without the shadow of a possibility of miscarrying. He inserted what is nothing less than a trip clause. He drafted a declaration which would force us, without any conceivable possibility of escape, evasion, mental reservation, or subterfuge of any kind, to execute the great sacrament of forgiveness in all its fullness and far-reaching power.

As we repeat the Great Prayer intelligently, considering and meaning what we say, we are suddenly, so to speak, caught up off our feet and grasped as though in a vise, so that we must face this problem—and there is no escape. We must positively and definitely extend forgiveness to everyone to whom it is possible that we can owe forgiveness, namely, to anyone who we think can have injured us in any way. Jesus leaves no room for any possible glossing of this fundamental thing. He has constructed his Prayer with more skill than ever yet lawyer displayed in the casting of a deed. He has so contrived it that once our attention has been drawn to this matter, we are inevitably obliged either to forgive our enemies in sincerity and truth, or never again to repeat that Prayer. It is safe to say that no one who reads this essay with understanding will ever again be able to use the Lord's Prayer unless and until he has forgiven. Should you now attempt to repeat it without forgiving, it can safely be predicted that you will not be able to finish it. This great central clause will stick in your throat.

Notice that Jesus does not say, "forgive me my trespasses and I will try to forgive others," or "I will see if it can be done," or "I will forgive generally, with certain exceptions." He obliges us to declare that we have actually forgiven, and forgiven all, *and he makes our claim to our own forgiveness to depend upon that.* Who is there who has grace enough to say his prayers at all, who does not long for the forgiveness or cancellation of his own mistakes and faults. Who would be so insane as to endeavor to seek the Kingdom of God without desiring to be relieved of his own sense of guilt. No one, we may believe. And so we see that we are trapped in the inescapable position that we cannot demand our own release before we have released our brother.

The forgiveness of others is the vestibule of Heaven, and Jesus knew it, and has led us to the door. You must forgive everyone who has ever hurt you if you want to be forgiven yourself; that is the long and the short of it. You have to get rid of all resentment and condemnation of others, and, not least, of self-condemnation and remorse. You have to forgive others, and having discontinued your own mistakes, you have to accept the forgiveness of God for them too, or you cannot make any progress. You have to forgive yourself, but you cannot forgive yourself sincerely until you have forgiven others first. Having forgiven others, you must be prepared to forgive yourself too, for to refuse to forgive oneself is only spiritual pride. "And by that sin fell the angels." We cannot make this point too clear to ourselves; we have got to forgive. There are few people in the world who have not at some time or other been hurt, really hurt, by someone else; or been disappointed, or injured, or deceived, or misled. Such things sink into the memory where they usually cause inflamed and festering wounds, and there is only one remedy—they have to be plucked out and thrown away. And the one and only way to do that is by forgiveness.

Of course, nothing in all the world is easier than to forgive people who have not hurt us very much. Nothing is easier than to rise above the thought of a trifling loss. Anybody will be willing to do this, but what the Law of Being requires of us is that we forgive not only these trifles, but the very things that are so hard to forgive that at first it seems impossible to do it at all. The despairing heart cries, "It is too much to ask. That thing meant too much to me. It is impossible. I cannot forgive it." But the Lord's Prayer makes our own forgiveness from God, which means our escape from guilt and limitation, dependent upon just this very thing. There is no escape from this, and so forgiveness there must be, no matter how deeply we may have been injured, or how terribly we have suffered. It must be done.

If your prayers are not being answered, search your consciousness and see if there is not someone whom you have yet to forgive. Find out if there is not some old thing about which you are very resentful. Search and see if you are not really holding a grudge (it may be camouflaged in some self-righteous way) against some individual, or some body of people, a nation, a race, a social class, some religious movement of which you disapprove perhaps, a political party, or what-not.

If you are doing so, then you have an act of forgiveness to perform, and when this is done, you will probably make your demonstration. If you cannot forgive at present, you will have to wait for your demonstration until you can, and you will have to postpone finishing your recital of the Lord's Prayer too, or involve yourself in the position that you do not desire the forgiveness of God.

Setting others free means setting yourself free, because resentment is really a form of attachment. It is a cosmic truth that it takes two to make a prisoner; the prisoner—and a gaoler. There is no such thing as being a prisoner on one's own account. Every prisoner must have a gaoler, and the gaoler is as much a prisoner as his charge. When you hold resentment against anyone, you are bound to that person by a cosmic link, a real, though mental chain. You are tied by a cosmic tie to the thing that you hate. The one person perhaps in the whole world whom you most dislike is the very one to whom you are attaching yourself by a hook that is stronger than steel. Is this what you wish? Is this the condition in which you desire to go on living? Remember, you belong to the thing with which you are linked in thought, and at some time or other, if that tie endures, the object of your resentment will be drawn again into your life, perhaps to work further havoc. Do you think that you can afford this? Of course, no one can afford such a thing; and so the way is clear. You must cut all such ties, by a clear and spiritual act of forgiveness. You must loose him and let him go. By forgiveness you set yourself free; you save your soul. And because the law of love works alike for one and all, you help to save his soul too, making it just so much easier for him to become what he ought to be.

But how, in the name of all that is wise and good, is the magic act of forgiveness to be accomplished, when we have been so deeply injured that, though we have long wished with all our hearts that we could forgive, we have nevertheless found it impossible; when we have tried and tried to forgive, but have found the task beyond us.

The technique of forgiveness is simple enough, and not very difficult to manage when you understand how. The only thing that is essential is *willingness* to forgive. Provided you desire to forgive the offender, the greater part of the work is already done. People have always made such a bogey of forgiveness because they have been under the erroneous impression that to forgive a person means that you have to compel yourself to like him. Happily this is by no means the case—we are not called upon to like anyone whom we do not find ourselves liking spontaneously, and, indeed, it is quite impossible to like people to order. You can no more *like* to order than you can hold the winds in your fist, and if you endeavor to coerce yourself into doing so, you will finish by disliking or hating the offender more than ever. People used to think that when someone had hurt them very much, it was their duty, as good Christians, to pump up, as it were, a feeling of liking for him; and since such a thing is utterly impossible, they suffered a great deal of distress, and ended, necessarily, with failure, and a resulting sense of sinfulness. We are not obliged to like anyone; but we are under a binding obligation to love everyone, love, or charity as the Bible calls it, meaning a vivid sense of impersonal good will. This has nothing directly to do with the feelings, though it is always *followed*, sooner or later, by a wonderful feeling of peace and happiness.

The method of forgiving is this: Get by yourself and become quiet. Repeat any prayer or treatment that appeals to you, or read a chapter of the Bible. Then quietly say, "I fully and freely forgive X (mentioning the name of the offender); I loose him and let him go. I completely forgive the whole business in question. As far as I am concerned, it is finished forever, I cast the burden of resentment upon the Christ within me. He is free now, and I am free too. I wish him well in every phase of his life. That incident is finished. The Christ Truth has set us both free. I thank God." Then get up and go about your business. On no account repeat this act of forgiveness, because you have done it once and for all, and to do it a second time would be tacitly to repudiate your own work. Afterward, whenever the memory of the offender or offense happens to come into your mind, bless the delinquent briefly and dismiss the thought. Do this, however many times the thought may come back. After a few days it will return less and less often, until you forget it altogether. Then, perhaps after an interval, shorter or longer, the old trouble may come back to memory once more, but you will find that now all bitterness and resentment have disappeared, and you are both free with the perfect freedom of the children of God. Your forgiveness is complete. You will experience a wonderful joy in the realization of the demonstration.

Everybody should practice general forgiveness every day as a matter of course. When you say your daily prayers, issue a general amnesty, forgiving everyone who may have injured you in any way, and on no account particularize. Simply say: "I freely forgive everyone." Then in the course of the day, should the thought of grievance or resentment come up, bless the offender briefly and dismiss the thought.

The result of this policy will be that very soon you will find yourself cleared of all resentment and condemnation, and the effect upon your happiness, your bodily health, and your general life will be nothing less than revolutionary.

Lead us not into temptation; but deliver us from evil

This cause has probably caused more difficulty than any other part of the Prayer. For many earnest people it has been a veritable stumbling block. They feel, and rightly, that God could not lead anyone into temptation or into evil in any circumstances, and so these words do not ring true.

For this reason, a number of attempts have been made to recast the wording. People have felt that Jesus could not have said what he is represented to have said, and so they look about for some phrasing which they think would be more in accordance with the general tone of his teaching. Heroic efforts have been made to wrest the Greek original into something different. All this, however, is unnecessary. The Prayer in the form in which we have it in English gives a perfectly correct sense of the true inner meaning. Remember that the Lord's Prayer covers the whole of the spiritual life. Condensed though the form is, it is nevertheless a complete manual for the development of the soul, and Jesus knew only too well the subtle perils and difficulties that can and do beset the soul when once the preliminary stages of spiritual unfoldment have been passed. Because those who are yet at a comparatively early stage of development do not experience such difficulties, they are apt to jump to the conclusion that this clause is unnecessary; but such is not the case.

The facts are these—the more you pray, the more time you spend in meditation and spiritual treatment, the more sensitive you become. And if you spend a great deal of time working on your soul in the right way, you will become very sensitive. This is excellent; but like everything in the universe, it works both ways. The more sensitive and spiritual you become, the more powerful and effective are your prayers, you do better healing, and you advance rapidly. But, for the same reason, you also become susceptible to forms of temptation that simply do not beset those at an earlier stage. You will also find that for ordinary faults, even things that many men and women of the world would consider to be trifling, you will be sharply punished, and this is well, because it keeps you up to the mark. The seemingly minor transgressions, the "little foxes that spoil the vines," would fritter away our spiritual power if not promptly dealt with.

No one at this level will be tempted to pick a pocket, or burgle a house, but this does not by any means imply that one will not have difficulties, and because of their subtlety, even greater difficulties, to meet.

As we advance, new and powerful temptations await us on the Path, ever ready to hurl us down if we are not watchful—temptations to work for self-glory, and self-aggrandizement instead of for God; for personal honors and distinctions, even for material gain; temptations to allow personal preferences to hold sway in our counsels when it is a sacred duty to deal with all men in perfect impartiality. Above and beyond all other sins the deadly sin of spiritual pride, truly "the last infirmity of noble mind," lurks on this road. Many fine souls who have triumphantly surmounted all other testings have lapsed into a condition of superiority and self-righteousness that has fallen like a curtain of steel between them and God. Great knowledge brings great responsibility. Great responsibility betrayed brings terrible punishment in its train. *Noblesse oblige* is preeminently true in spiritual things. One's knowledge of the Truth, however little it may be, is a sacred trust for humanity that must not be violated. While we should never make the mistake of casting our pearls before swine, nor urge the Truth in quarters where it is not welcome, yet we must do all that we wisely can to spread the true knowledge of God among mankind, that not one of "these little ones" may go hungry through our selfishness or our neglect. "Feed my lambs, feed my sheep."

The old occult writers were so vividly sensible of these dangers that, with their instinct for dramatization, they spoke of the soul as being challenged by various tests as it traversed the upward road. It was as though the traveller were halted at various gates or turnpike bars, and tested by some ordeal to determine whether he were ready to advance any further. If he succeeded in passing the test, they said, he was allowed to continue upon his way with the blessing of the challenger. If, however, he failed to survive the ordeal, he was forbidden to proceed.

Now, some less experienced souls, eager for rapid advancement, have rashly desired to be subjected immediately to all kinds of tests, and have even looked about, seeking for difficulties to overcome; as though one's own personality did not already present quite enough material for any one man or woman to deal with. Forgetting the lesson of our Lord's own ordeal in the wilderness, forgetting the injunction "Thou shalt not tempt the Lord thy God," they have virtually done this very thing, with sad results. And so Jesus has inserted this clause, in which we pray that we may not have to meet anything that is too much for us at the present level of our understanding. And, if we are wise, and work daily, as we should, for wisdom, understanding, purity, and the guidance of the Holy Spirit, we never shall find ourselves in any difficulty for which we have not the understanding necessary to clear ourselves. *Nothing shall by any means hurt you. Behold I am with you always.*

Thine is the kingdom, and the power, and the glory, for ever and ever

This is a wonderful gnomic saying summing up the essential truth of the Omnipresence and the Allness of God. It means that God is indeed All in All, the doer, the doing, and the deed, and one can say also the spectator. The Kingdom in this sense means all creation, on every plane, for that is the Presence of God—God as manifestation or expression.

The Power, of course, is the Power of God. We know that God is the only power, and so, when we work, as when we pray, it is really God doing it by means of us. Just as the pianist produces his music by means of, or through his fingers, so may mankind be thought of as the fingers of God. His is the Power. If, when you are praying, you hold the thought that it is really God who is working through you, your prayers will gain immeasurably in efficiency. Say, "God is inspiring me." If, when you have any ordinary thing to do, you hold the thought, "Divine Intelligence is working through me now," you will perform the most difficult tasks with astonishing success.

The wondrous change that comes over us as we gradually realize what the Omnipresence of God really means, transfigures every phase of our lives, turning sorrow into joy, age into youth, and dullness into light and life. This is the glory—and the glory which comes to us is, of course, God's too. And the bliss we know in that experience is still God Himself, who is knowing that bliss through us.

In recent years, the Lord's Prayer has often been rewritten in the affirmative form. In this style, for instance, the clause "Thy kingdom come, thy will be done," becomes, "Thy kingdom is come, thy will is being done." All such paraphrases are interesting and suggestive, but their importance is not vital. The affirmative form of prayer should be used for all healing work, but it is only one form of prayer. Jesus used the invocatory form very often, though not always, and the frequent use of this form is essential to the growth of the soul. It is not to be confused with supplicatory prayer, in which the subject begs and whines to God as a slave pleading with his master. That is always wrong. The highest of all forms of prayer is true contemplation, in which the thought and the thinker become one. This is the Unity of the mystic, but it is rarely experienced in the earliest stages. Pray in whatever way you find easiest; for the easiest way is the best.

Come unto me all ye that labor and are heavy laden and I will give you rest.

The Lord is my light and my salvation; whom shall I fear? The Lord is the strength of my life; of whom shall I be afraid?
Though an host should encamp against me, my heart shall not fear: though war should rise against me, in this will I be confident.

When thou passest through the waters, I will be with thee; and through the rivers, they shall not overflow thee: when thou walkest through fire, thou shalt not be burned; neither shall the flame kindle upon thee.

As long as he sought the Lord, God made him to prosper.

1. The Lord is my shepherd; I shall not want.

2. He maketh me to lie down in green pastures: he leadeth me beside the still waters.

3. He restoreth my soul: he leadeth me in the paths of righteousness for his name's sake.

4. Yea, though I walk through the valley of the shadow of death, I will fear no evil: for thou art with me; thy rod and thy staff they comfort me.

5. Thou preparest a table before me in the presence of mine enemies: thou anointest my head with oil; my cup runneth over.

6. Surely goodness and mercy shall follow me all the days of my life: and I will dwell in the house of the Lord for ever.

The Good Shepherd

A MEDITATION ON PSALM 23

The Twenty-third Psalm is a spiritual treatment in
the form of a poem.
You should read this meditation through several
times, dwelling on each statement and endeavoring
to realize the significance of what you are reading.

THE Lord Is My Shepherd. The Lord
means God, in particular my own
knowledge of Truth, as that knowledge is the Presence of God in me, my indwelling
Christ. This is my shepherd. The shepherd takes care
of his sheep, and the Lord will take care of me because
I am now seeking Him through this meditation. I have
only to realize sufficiently this Truth, that the Lord is
my shepherd, and every negative thing in my life will
vanish away.

I Shall Not Want. I really believe this, and I fully accept it, so I am not going to be afraid of anything. I
firmly believe that I shall not want for any good
thing.

He *Maketh Me to Lie Down in Green Pastures.* Green
pastures symbolize an abundance of all good things
that I need, and perfect all-round harmony in my life.
They are to be mine permanently and forever, and

not merely as a temporary demonstration; that is why I may be said to lie down in them.

He Leadeth Me Beside the Still Waters. Water in the Bible symbolizes the soul. To lead me beside the still waters means that the power of God in prayer sets my soul at rest, giving me perfect peace. I know that when once my soul is at peace my demonstration *must* come, and that my only task is to bring about this peace. By this meditation I am practicing the Presence of God. That is, I am praying for peace, and I know that this prayer will be answered.

He Restoreth My Soul. This is my promise of complete salvation. My prayer is now being answered. The peace of God is filling my soul. All my difficulties have arisen from my soul having separated herself in belief from her Living Source. I have thought myself to be separated from God, and, therefore, for practical purposes, I was separated, and this has meant for me a load of responsibility, selfishness, fear, and limitation; in other words, the "Fall of Man." This text, however, definitely promises the restoration of my soul to her original Divine understanding, and is a guarantee of freedom. I affirm that this is now true. I claim full salvation from all my difficulties. I claim perfect health, happiness, and prosperity. I am free.

He Leadeth Me in the Paths of Righteousness for His Name's Sake. Righteousness means right thinking, and I know that to think rightly about any condition means healing and safety. All evil is wrong thought, all good is right or true thought. Christ in me, my Good Shepherd, is now guiding me in the path of Right Thought; so all will be well. In the Bible "the name" of anything is the nature or character of that thing. The nature of God is all-powerful, omnipresent good, boundless love. I know that this Boundless Love is now taking care of me, and arranging my affairs.

Yea, Though I Walk Through the Valley of the Shadow of Death, I will Fear No Evil: for Thou Art with Me. I am never again going to be afraid of anything, because Thou, my Good Shepherd, art with me. I know that Thou who art all Love, and hast all Power, protectest me, and that we are One forever and forever. I know that I never can find myself anywhere but Thou wilt be there too. I know that because Thou art Life, there is no death, and I note that the Bible speaks not of death, but of the *shadow* of death, which is our false belief. There is no death, but the seeming loss of Thy Presence.

Thy Rod and Thy Staff They Comfort Me. I know that Thy Law changeth not, because Thou art Divine Principle, and I know that my word shall go forth in this meditation, and that it shall not return unto me void, because I am Thy child and the heir of Thy Kingdom.

Thou Preparest a Table before Me in the Presence of Mine Enemies. My enemies are my own thoughts: my doubts, my fears, my thoughts of criticism of others, and self-condemnation—the only enemies I can have. "A man's enemies shall be those of his own household." But these now no longer have any power to hurt me because I am speaking the Word of Truth, and my Good Shepherd will bring me a glorious demonstration in the teeth of every difficulty.

Thou Anointest My Head with Oil. In the Bible, oil and ointment are symbols of gladness, praise, and thanksgiving. This line assures me that I am to be rescued from all my difficulties. Anointing with oil is also a symbol of consecration, and by meditating in this way on the Truth, I am reconsecrated as the perfect child of God. I bless God for His perfect goodness. I thank God for His perfect, unceasing care for me. I praise Him for the glory of His Name. I thank Him in particular for a perfect and generous demonstration over my present difficulties.

My Cup Runneth Over. This is an additional assurance of the thoroughness and fullness of my demonstration; not simply that God will rescue me from my difficulties, but that I am going to receive a clear, full, and all-satisfying solution of my problem, and of the unseen causes underlying it, so that it will disappear forever out of my life. When my Good Shepherd replenishes my cup, it is not merely filled; it runs over.

Surely Goodness and Mercy Shall Follow Me All the Days of My Life. Because I know that every good prayer should finish with thanksgiving and a declaration of faith, I now give Thee thanks, Infinite Divine Love, for the accomplished fact, and I praise Thy glorious, unbounded perfection, for the flawless harmony, and peace, and triumph that shall surely be mine. I affirm this triumph. I claim it. I appropriate it. It is mine.

I Will Dwell in the House of the Lord For Ever. Thank God that I now know indeed that the Lord is my Shepherd, and that I never shall want for any good thing. I know it and realize it. My soul is rooted and grounded in Truth. Thy Presence is with me and it gives me rest. Now no fear nor doubts can by any means creep in. I am Thy child, the Son of Thy House, a house not made with hands, Eternal in the Heaven, and in that house I dwell with Thee forever and ever.

It is Finished. All is Well.

1. He that dwelleth in the secret place of the most High shall abide under the shadow of the Almighty.

2. I will say of the Lord, he is my refuge and my fortress: my God; in him will I trust.

3. Surely he shall deliver thee from the snare of the fowler, and from the noisome pestilence.

4. He shall cover thee with his feathers, and under his wings shalt thou trust: his truth shall be thy shield and buckler.

5. Thou shalt not be afraid for the terror by night; nor for the arrow that flieth by day;

6. Nor for the pestilence that walketh in darkness; nor for the destruction that wasteth at noonday.

7. A thousand shall fall at thy side, and ten thousand at thy right hand; but it shall not come nigh thee.

8. Only with thine eyes shalt thou behold and see the reward of the wicked.

9. Because thou has made the Lord, which is my refuge, even the most High, thy habitation;

10. There shall no evil befall thee, neither shall any plague come nigh thy dwelling.

11. For he shall give his angels charge over thee, to keep thee in all thy ways.

12. They shall bear thee up in their hands, lest thou dash thy foot against a stone.

13. Thou shalt tread upon the lion and adder: the young lion and the dragon shalt thou trample under feet.

14. Because he hath set his love upon me, therefore will I deliver him: I will set him on high, because he hath known my name.

15. He shall call upon me, and I will answer him: I will be with him in trouble; I will deliver him, and honour him.

16. With long life will I satisfy him, and shew him my salvation.

The Secret Place

T HE Ninety-first Psalm is one of the very greatest chapters in the whole Bible. It is one of those chapters that everybody knows by heart. Yet, like so many familiar Bible passages, it is unfortunately among the least understood. It must, of course, be interpreted in the spiritual way, and it is only thus that the true meaning is arrived at. Like the rest of Scripture, the underlying thought is developed through a series of symbols, and it is by the appreciation of the values lying behind these that the power of this prayer is appropriated.

The Book of Psalms has been called "The Little Bible," and it certainly forms a matchless treasure-house of spiritual riches. This wonderful collection of poems, lyrical, dramatic, elegiac, contains something to fit every mood, and to meet every need of humanity. All through the centuries of both Old Testament and Christian history, they have been a never failing source of inspiration and comfort for men and women of every kind and every walk of life, and it is safe to say that no soul in need has ever turned to the Book of Psalms in vain.

The Ninety-first Psalm when scientifically understood, is found to be one of the most powerful prayers ever written. All sorts of people have got themselves out of every conceivable kind of trouble working on this prayer every day, in the spiritual way. Other cases are on record of people who had not prayed for years turning to this prayer in some great emergency and overcoming their difficulty; with only the surface meaning to help them. It will easily be seen, therefore, how well worth while it is to make oneself thoroughly acquainted with at least the principal ideas contained within it, for then one has always ready to hand a practical prayer of unparalleled power.

The best way to get the most out of this psalm is to read it through quietly; pause after each clause to consider the meaning as given in the commentary; assent to this mentally; and then pass on to the next. Remember that all this is praying. Prayer is, essentially, thinking about God—not necessarily addressing God, helpful though this may be at times—and while you are working on this psalm, analyzing the text, and considering the meaning in your own mind, you are praying, and in a very efficient way too. If you are in a specific difficulty, and particularly if you are rather fearful, you will find, after working through the prayer once or twice or perhaps three times, that most of your fear will have gone, and that you are now looking at things from a different point of view—and this is the change in mentality that brings about results.

Let us then consider the prayer in detail, taking it verse by verse.

He that dwelleth in the secret place of the most High shall abide under the shadow of the Almighty. The Secret Place of the Most High is your own consciousness, and this fact is the most important practical discovery in the whole science of religion. The error that is usually made is to suppose the Secret Place of the Most High to be somewhere outside of yourself; across the sea, or up in the sky probably. This error is usually fatal to our hopes, because our prospects of success in prayer depend upon our succeeding in getting some degree of contact with God, and since He is only to be contacted within, and never without, as long as we are looking without we must naturally fail in our objective. Jesus emphasized this truth again and again; indeed it is the foundation-stone of his whole teaching. "Seek first the Kingdom of God," he said, and, when asked where that kingdom could be found, replied, "The Kingdom of God is within you." And again he said that when we pray we are to enter into the closet and shut the door, meaning, to retire in thought within our own consciousness and to withdraw our attention from outer things. In fact, this doctrine of the Secret Place and the wonders that can happen therein is taught right throughout the Bible.

To abide under the shadow of the Almighty means to live under the protection of God Himself. "Under the shadow," is a dramatic, Oriental expression for safety. Eastern people, and especially those with a desert background, such as the people of Palestine, look upon the sun as a danger, even an enemy, from which they need to be safeguarded. In the West, as a rule, we look upon him as our greatest friend, and we can hardly get enough sun to satisfy us; but in the East it is otherwise. There, shade is sanctuary, or safety—"the shadow of a great rock in a weary land." The exhausted traveller, on attaining his goal, sinks down in the shade for his long-sought rest, feeling that now at last he is safe.

Let us note that here God is called "The Almighty," this title being selected from among the many other titles that the Bible has for God, in order to impress us at this point with the fact that He really is Almighty, and that He can therefore overcome our present difficulty for us, no matter how big it may seem at the moment—"With God all things are possible." Consider, however, that the promise is made to "him that *dwelleth*." If we only run into the Secret Place now and again when we are in trouble, we can scarcely be said to dwell there. God will always come to our rescue *whenever* we pray, but if we seldom think of Him at other times, we may experience considerable difficulty in making our contact in an emergency; or we may even be so perturbed as to forget altogether to pray. By means of regular daily prayer and meditation we dwell in the Secret Place, and then we may expect to abide under the shadow, and to enjoy the protection of the Power that is indeed All Powerful.

At this point we notice a change in the form of the psalm from the third person to the first. This is a literary stroke of rare skill. Observe that the poem opens by definitely announcing the irresistible power of prayer. It states a general Cosmic Law in a form of scientific detachment. In order to bring home to you with unmistakable clearness the fact that this law applies to you, as much as to anything or anyone in the universe, and that by no possibility could you be an exception, it now changes over to the first person and makes you say "I." In the language of metaphysics, it compels you to voice the I AM.

I will say of the Lord, He is my refuge and my fortress: my God; in Him will I trust. The Lord means God, in particular your own knowledge of Truth, as that knowledge is in itself the Presence of God in the one who knows it, his Indwelling Christ. How can knowledge be a presence? Secular knowledge, which is intellectual, cannot; but the true knowledge of God is not an intellectual theory; it is an actual experience—not a thing of the head, but of the heart—and this is indeed a Presence. It is indeed one's own higher, or Real Self. It is pure Spirit. It is at one with God. As a general rule, people contact this Real Self only vaguely and occasionally at first, often calling the experience "intuition." Then, if they pray regularly in the scientific way, and especially if they frequently pray for inspiration, the flickering gleams of intuition gradually magnify and strengthen into a clear and definite sense of the Presence of God, when He really becomes their Lord. The student should understand, however, that it is by no means necessary to get this clear sense of the Divine Presence in order to have the help of God. The very fact that you are praying at all means that the action of God is taking place in your consciousness, and the action of God must have results.

In Him will I trust. However worried or depressed you may be, however full of doubts and misgivings, still the very fact that you are praying means that you have at least enough faith for that. The faith to go on praying in the midst of doubts about results is the tiny grain of mustard seed that Jesus says is sufficient for practical purposes. "In Him will I trust" is an expression of your determination to trust in God in spite of appearances. It means that you have now determined to trust practically in God by ceasing to worry and fear. This is the legitimate and spiritual use of the will. Your will is a Divine faculty, and has its own place in the spiritual life. Of course, the will can be misused. We must not try to bring events to pass by the direct exertion of will power, even to produce a bodily healing;

but the will must be employed to say whether we are going to pray or not to pray; whether we are going to give way to fear or to refuse to do so; whether we are going to yield to temptation or not. In the case of temptation, it is notorious how often will power fails, but that is because the will should be employed, not to fight the temptation directly, but to choose to pray about it instead of giving way to it.

This phrase means, not that you have already attained a sense of security, but that—though you still feel yourself to be in danger—you are choosing by the correct exercise of your power of will to put your trust in the Love of God, instead of in the impending danger.

At this point the poem dramatically changes again, this time from the first person to the second. You have now voiced the I AM; you have recognized both the power and the goodness of God; and the fact of the living Presence of God in you and with you. You have determined, by a spiritual act of will, to trust in God, and by this procedure you have brought the action of God into play in your life. You have done your part. Now the Word of Truth is represented as addressing you with an authoritative assurance that your prayer will be answered, that in some way or other—not by any means necessarily in the way that you expect, but in some good way—you will be rescued from your difficulty. Again the Eastern instinct for dramatic form drives the great truth home with unequalled power in this employment of the second person.

Surely He shall deliver thee from the snare of the fowler, and from the noisome pestilence. He shall cover thee with His feathers, and under His wings shalt thou trust: His truth shall be thy shield and buckler. Needless to say, both the

fowler's snare and the noisome pestilence are to be
interpreted in the most general sense as including any
kind of danger, material, moral, or spiritual, that can
threaten your welfare; and very apt descriptions they
are of many of the perils that beset the children of
men in their daily round. You are, however, to have
no apprehension, for your protection is now assured
to you in one of those beautiful illustrations from simple everyday life in which the Bible abounds. What
child has not watched with delight the familiar farm-
yard scene in which the motherly old hen, at the
slightest threat of danger, gathers the little chicks
under her wings, covering them "with her feathers,"
from any possible harm. Thus does God shield you
from all danger once you have elected to trust Him.
His truth shall be thy shield and buckler. It is the knowledge of the Truth about God and man that makes the
demonstration. One does not *do* something with Divine Truth; it is the knowing of that Truth that in itself
heals the condition. *Ye shall know the truth, and the truth
shall make you free.*

*Thou shalt not be afraid for the terror by night; nor for the
arrow that flieth by days; Nor for the pestilence that walketh
in darkness; nor for the destruction that wasteth at noonday.*
These two verses together with verse 13, lower down,
constitute a superb analysis of the rationale of man's
psychological nature. The respective characteristics of
our conscious and subconscious minds are contrasted
with unsurpassed insight. For practical purposes, all
our troubles may be classified as belonging to either
the conscious or the subconscious mind, and have to
be dealt with accordingly. The arrow that flieth by day
and the destruction that wasteth at noon refer to any
difficulty of which you are consciously aware, whether

that difficulty be a physical ailment, a business problem, trouble with another person, or what-not. The
point here is that you are aware of the difficulty, and
that you are seeking in one way or another to overcome it. It is, so to say, a daytime problem.

The terror by night and the pestilence that walketh
in darkness, on the contrary, imply something that, unknown to you, is working in your subconscious mind,
or, unsuspected by you in the world outside of yourself. Modern psychology has shown conclusively that
most of our difficulties have their roots far out of sight
in the depths of the subconscious, and that these subconscious minds, in fact, contain an enormous amount
of material whose presence we little suspect. These are
indeed terrors of the mental night and pestilences of
the darkness. In a less personal sense, they refer to any
danger from outside of yourself of which you may be
unaware. An impending accident, for instance, would
come under this heading, or any hostile activities by
people secretly inimical to you. If, let us say, an enemy
were covertly working against you, or, as occasionally
happens, a business partner or an employee were acting to your detriment, unsuspected by you, such things
would come under this heading of hidden trouble.

*A thousand shall fall at thy side, and ten thousand at thy
right hand; but it shall not come nigh thee. Only with thine
eyes shalt thou behold and see the reward of the wicked.* This
clause has been gravely misunderstood. It has been
taken to indicate some kind of favoritism on the part
of God, whereas, of course, such a thing is utterly impossible. "No respecter of persons." It really means,
quite simply, that prayer does change things, that those
who pray are saved from trouble that would otherwise
overtake them, and that does, in fact, overtake those

who do not pray. The word "wicked" originally meant bewitched, and the wicked need not necessarily be conscious wrongdoers, but are much more frequently just those who do not rely upon God, or trouble to say their prayers, because they are bewitched or deceived by materialism, or atheism, or by simple doubt in the efficacy of prayer. Because they do not pray they cannot expect to escape from trouble and do not succeed in doing so.

Because thou hast made the Lord, which is my refuge, even the most High, thy habitation; There shall no evil befall thee, neither shall any plague come nigh thy dwelling. This is one of the most definite and concrete promises given in the whole Bible. In all the many declarations of the nearness and certainty of God's help, which abound in the Scriptures, not one is more precise or more definite than this. It says that once you have made this Divine Christ Power your refuge, by living regularly in the spiritual consciousness—making it your habitation—no trouble can touch you. Could the thing possibly be more pointedly and convincingly stated?

The Bible has an idiom that is all its own, and in this idiom the word "promise" is the name given to a statement of some metaphysical law. It is not used in the sense in which you promise a person to do something at some future date, meaning an agreement or pledge. Such a promise is supposed to be a matter of choice on the part of its author who says in effect, "I am willing to do such a thing next week or next year. I choose now to agree to do it." Thus one may promise to pay a sum of money in six months' time, or one may promise a child to take it to a show next week. A Bible "promise" is a statement of a natural law in metaphysics, just as a "law" of physics such as Boyle's law or Ohm's law is a statement of the consequences, upon the physical plane, that will naturally follow upon certain other occurrences.

So, a Bible "promise" is a statement of the consequences that naturally follow from certain thoughts and states of consciousness. If Boyle's law were written in the Bible idiom, it would read something like this: "As I live, saith the Lord, whenever thou shalt double the pressure of a gas, thou shalt halve the volume, temperature remaining constant." In the language of natural science, our Bible promise would run: "By meditating regularly on the Presence of God with you, and directing your life in accordance with that fact, you become immune from any kind of danger."

For He shall give His angels charge over thee, to keep thee in all thy ways. They shall bear thee up in their hands, lest thou dash thy foot against a stone. This is one of the very loveliest of all the promises in the Bible. For tender beauty it stands alone. Re-read it carefully now, and ask yourself whether human language could possibly say anything more exquisite than this, or promise anything more wonderful. *He shall give His angels charge over thee to keep thee in all thy ways*—and it is meant for you and for me. It might have seemed appropriate that some extraordinary or exalted Being should be given an escort of angels, as a bodyguard, to support him, to keep him in all his ways. But the Bible is the book of Everyman, and this promise is given to you and to me.

It would be no bad thing if you made this single verse the subject of careful meditation every day for a month. If, in that way, you came to realize, however feebly, the real significance of this promise—that you are to be in the charge of angels and safeguarded in all your ways (not merely in certain ways, but in all your

ways); safeguarded for bodily health, for food, clothing, rent, and the other necessaries of life; for right activity and self-expression; for congenial companion-
ship; safeguarded from temptation and from fear as
well—what a staggering difference this would make in
your life.

*Thou shalt tread upon the lion and adder: the young lion
and the dragon shalt thou trample under feet.* Having sung
of the invincible protection and loving kindness of
God in this glorious burst of poetry, the inspired writer
now re-states the same idea from the scientific or psychological point of view. The great Illumined Ones
who wrote the Bible under Divine inspiration well
knew all the teaching of modern psychology. They understood human nature as no other teachers have ever
understood it, and they wrote of it in their own way as
no others have ever written of it before or since. The
ideas concerning the subconscious mind and the part
it plays in our scheme of things, which have lately been
put forward by investigators like Freud and Jung and
others, novel though they appear to the modern
world, were all quite familiar to the great Initiates of
the Bible—that is to say, the portions of these teachings which are correct, for, of course, they are on
many points at variance with fact. Moses, Isaiah, John,
and the author of this psalm, for example, knew all
that is to be known about the subconscious mind and
the way in which it functions. They knew all about
what we call complexes and neuroses, the unconscious
motive, the phenomena of dissociation and splitting,
and many other things too that our psychologists have
not yet discovered. Here the Psalmist draws a further
contrast between the subconscious danger and the
consciously realized difficulty, as a development of

verses 5 and 6. Now it is the adder and the dragon put against the lion. The lion stands for a difficulty about which we are informed; one of which we are so afraid that it seems a very lion in our path. The lion has his faults; he is indeed extraordinarily undesirable as a companion—ferocious, pitiless, quick as lightning, strong as steel; but credit he must be given for one major virtue—he is no sneak. He rushes at you in the open; you know what you have to meet, and can take your measures. How different, on the other hand, is the attack of the adder, or snake; for it is hidden. It creeps upon you in the dark, and ordinarily you have no sense of danger until the blow falls. You cannot fight this enemy squarely, because you cannot see it. Here, of course, we again recognize subconscious trouble, and in the repeated and parallel phrase so characteristic of Hebrew poetry the lion becomes a young or particularly vigorous lion, and the adder becomes a dragon, and this is the Bible term for what in modern psychology is called a complex. A complex is a group of ideas heavily charged with emotion and hidden away in the subconscious mind. These emotions usually have their roots in one of the great primary instincts of human nature, and this fact endows them with what is often a terribly destructive power.

And here you are promised that your complexes shall be dissolved by the Christ Truth, the realization of God. Utterly dissolved. Completely dispersed. *Trampled under feet,* is the telling phrase employed to express their complete annihilation. There is nothing that can be done by psycho-analysis or any other form of psycho-therapy that cannot be much better done by Scientific Prayer, or the Practice of the Presence of God. Prayer, which is the appeal to God, as distinct from any form of mere mental treatment, goes straight to the seat of the trouble, wherever it may be, without need of any direction on your part. When you pray about any specific difficulty, enough prayer will remove that difficulty by removing its real mental cause, whatever or wherever it may be, even though you do not in the least suspect the cause, or even though you may be erroneously attributing it to quite a wrong cause. However deep down in the subconscious life the trouble may be, the Christ Truth will find it and redeem it. *(He descended into hell.)*

The last three verses constitute the final stanza. They are in themselves a glorious psalm of ringing joy and triumph. Even when used alone, they form a complete and wonderful spiritual treatment. Here once more we find a dramatic change in the presentation, with the object of compelling you to voice the I AM on the highest note. Thus your simple prayer gradually develops into nothing less than the Logos, the creative Word of God, spoken through you.

Because he hath set his love upon me, therefore until I deliver him. This is one of those gnomic sayings in which the Bible abounds, where an ocean of teaching is crystallized into a phrase. It is a definite statement that you are to be delivered from your difficulty because you have set your love upon God. That, definitely and simply. There is nothing hypothetical or contingent here; no conditions whatever either expressed or implied. The statement indicates the accomplished fact—the fixed decision, as it were—*I will deliver him.* And why?—*because he hath set his love upon me.* "But, alas," you may say, "this cannot apply to me, because, to be honest, I do not really feel any very strong sense of love for God. How I should like to!—

but I do not." To which the answer is, that your love for God is not an emotion. It has really nothing to do with the feelings at all. In these matters emotion is too often misleading. We demonstrate and prove our love for God by praying, and by refusing to recognize error as having any power over us; by declining, out of loyalty to God, to accept anything less than the perfect harmony which is His Will. *If you love Me, keep My commandments.* By the very fact that you have been praying about a difficulty, going through this psalm, for instance, you have been setting your love upon God, no matter how depressed or how doubtful you may have felt. And, therefore, He will deliver you.

I will set him on high, because he hath known My Name. In the Bible the "name" of anything means the nature or character of that thing. Now the nature of God is perfect, omnipresent, all-powerful good, boundless love; and to "know" this is to be set on high above all your difficulties—that is, to be taken out of them, into freedom, security, and happiness. This is because, in Biblical language, to know a thing is not a mere intellectual apprehension, but involves a certain degree of understanding and realization. So we see that when we have, through our prayers, attained some real appreciation of the Allness of God, our troubles disappear.

The last two verses gather up, so to say, all the implications and promises of this most wonderful stanza, and present them to the fearful or doubting heart as a song of triumph; promising counsel, and guidance in perplexity, salvation in trouble, and a long and joyous career, culminating in complete spiritual triumph. *He shall call upon me, and I will answer him: I will be with him in trouble; I will deliver him, and honour him. With long life will I satisfy him, and shew him by salvation.*

1. God is our refuge and strength, a very present help in trouble.

2. Therefore will not we fear, though the earth be removed, and though the mountains be carried into the midst of the sea;

3. Though the waters thereof roar and be troubled, though the mountains shake with the swelling thereof. Selah.

4. There is a river, the streams whereof shall make glad the city of God, the holy place of the tabernacles of the most High.

5. God is in the midst of her; she shall not be moved: God shall help her, and that right early.

6. The heathen raged, the kingdoms were moved: he uttered his voice, the earth melted.

7. The Lord of hosts is with us; the God of Jacob is our refuge. Selah.

8. Come, behold the works of the Lord, what desolations he hath made in the earth.

9. He maketh wars to cease unto the end of the earth; he breaketh the bow, and cutteth the spear in sunder; he burneth the chariot in the fire.

10. Be still, and know that I am God: I will be exalted among the heathen, I will be exalted in the earth.

11. The Lord of hosts is with us; the God of Jacob is our refuge. Selah.

Be Still

PSALM 46

THE Bible teaches spiritual Truth in many different ways. It gives direct teaching about God, as clear and precise as any book on philosophy that ever was written. It expounds the Great Message indirectly through historical narrative and by means of biographical studies, for the Bible includes the most wonderful and interesting set of human biographies that ever was written. It contains an unmatched collection of essays and treatises on the nature of God, and the nature of man, the powers of the soul, and the meaning of life. Consider John's opening section in the Gospel, for instance, or the 11th chapter of Hebrews, or the 12th and 13th of Corinthians I, or the 5th, 6th, and 7th of Matthew, to name only a few. Each of these chapters in a different way gives direct and simple teaching of the Truth, unsurpassed in any work outside of the Bible.

But it is in its prayers and treatments that the Bible is transcendent. It contains a large number of the greatest prayers ever written—beginning, of course, with what we call the "Lord's Prayer"—prayers the like of which have never been found elsewhere, for they go right down to the depths of the human soul, meeting every need that can arise, and providing for every possible temperament and any conceivable contingency—in fact they cater to "all sorts and conditions of men."

Among all the beautiful and heart searching prayers of the Bible there is none that surpasses the wonderful poem that we call the Forty-sixth Psalm. This is an inspired treatment that will enable you to overcome any kind of difficulty; if you can tune yourself in to the level of consciousness to which it attains. It is the supreme Bible treatment against fear.

Now the object of prayer or treatment is just this very raising of the consciousness, and a good prayer is the instrument that enables us to do it. We need not expect to begin our prayer with a realization. If we already had a realization we should not be needing the help of the prayer; we do not need a step-ladder to reach a height on which we are already placed. The ladder is employed in order to enable us to raise ourselves, step by step, to a height above the ground to which our muscles alone would never carry us; and so a good prayer is a step-ladder upon which we may gradually climb from the low level of fear, doubt, and difficulty, to the spiritual height where these things melt away in the Light of Truth.

Our psalm begins, as do nearly all the Bible prayers, with an expression of faith in God. This is extremely important in practice. You need to affirm constantly that you do believe in God, not merely as a vague abstract concept, but as a real, vivid, actual power in life, always available to be contacted in thought; never changing and never failing. It cannot be too strongly emphasized that it is not sufficient to take this for granted. It is not sufficient to accept the Truth once and for all, or once a week; you must continually reaffirm it in thought, and in words if necessary. You must constantly remind yourself that you do accept this position, that you believe in it, and that your conviction is good enough to build your life and your hopes upon. All this is treatment, and very powerful treatment too. It is treatment that really changes the soul by clearing out those subconscious fears that are the cause of all your difficulties.

And so the inspired writer starts his prayer by saying, bluntly, *God is our refuge and strength, a very present help in trouble*. You will see that he allows himself no doubts at all about this. He does not dream of taking up the timid, almost apologetic, attitude that some modern divines seem to think appropriate in dealing with God. He says firmly that God IS, that He exists indeed; and then he enumerates three facts concerning God. He says that He is our refuge; he says that He is our strength; and he says that He is "a very present help in trouble." This verse is really tremendous, is it not? If we get through the crust of familiarity that tends to hide the real meaning from us, and study these words with a fresh mind, we shall be amazed, I think, at all that they imply. Note that he says that God is our refuge. He does not say that such may very well be the case, or that it is a pious hope upon which we are justified in leaning; but that, plain and plump, God is our refuge.

Now pause a moment to consider all that God is. Review briefly, at this point, the principal aspects and attributes of God as you know them, and then consider that this Infinite Being is our refuge. That is to say, this Unlimited Power of Wisdom and Love is a refuge to which we can go in any kind of difficulty. Many devout souls have thought of God as a distant potentate dwelling in the skies, to be dreaded and feared; but the Bible says on the contrary that God is a refuge for those in difficulty. It then says that this Omnipotent Power is nothing less than our strength. This brings the idea home still more vividly. God is not merely a matchless power that will come to our rescue, but He will actually be our own strength, operating through us to the overcoming of difficulty when we call upon Him in the right way.

Every student of Truth must understand that God always acts *through* us by changing our consciousness.

We learn in divine metaphysics that God never does anything *to* us, or *for* us, but always *through* us. The writer drives these points home in the familiar Bible manner by adding, "a very present help in trouble."

The opening affirmation is followed, in the most scientific way, by an excellent example of the use of what is called in metaphysics the "denial." The next two verses are a denial that there is any power in conditions to make us be, or do, or submit to, anything short of the complete all-round harmony that is the Divine Will for us all. It says *therefore will not we fear*—as following logically upon our opening affirmation—*though the earth be removed, and though the mountains be carried into the midst of the sea; Though the waters thereof roar and be troubled, though the mountains shake with the swelling thereof.*

The "earth," of course, means manifestation. It is the Bible's term for all one's manifestation, or expression—the body, the home, the business life, relatives and associates, all come under the heading of the earth or the land. We know that all these outer things are but the expression of inner states of consciousness, and here the Psalmist makes us say that though the earth be removed, though all these outer things seem to go to pieces, our health break down, our money disappear, our friends desert us, yet we are not going to be afraid. This attitude is extraordinarily valuable.

When things are going wrong declare constantly that you are not going to be afraid or intimidated by any outer condition. The more afraid you find yourself, the more need is there for doing this. The most important time to say, "God is my refuge, I am not going to be afraid," is when your knees are knocking together.

The Psalmist says that though the mountains be carried into the midst of the sea, and the waters roll and tremble until the very mountains themselves seem to shake, he is not going to be afraid. The mountain, in the Bible, always means prayer, the uplifted consciousness, and this clause makes us declare that even when in the midst of our prayers things seem to get worse, so that the very prayers themselves are all but swamped by our terror, or doubt, or despair; yet we are going to hold on to the truth about God, knowing that even though it be after forty days, the waters will subside— if only we hold on to the thought of God. The waters, of course, are always the human personality, and more especially the emotions.

The man who wrote this, we will agree, had no small knowledge of the human heart, its difficulties, and its needs.

There is a river, the streams whereof shall make glad the city of God, the holy place of the tabernacles of the most High. This is the capital river mentioned several times in Scripture; the river of life that flows from the throne of God. It means the understanding of Truth that is verily the "Waters of Life" to those who attain it. The river as a symbol is rather interesting. Primarily it stands for purpose. A river means purpose because it is always going somewhere. A river does not stay in one place, like a lake, or even an ocean, but is always on the way to a destination. In this respect it is a true type of the dedicated life which every student of Divine Truth is supposed to be living. In this teaching, if it really means anything to us, we are no longer drifting about like a log at the mercy of the ride, but are definitely headed along the pathway of understanding and freedom.

"The City of God" is man's consciousness. Your consciousness, which is your identity in life, is called a "city" in the Bible. "Except the Lord keep the city, the watchman waketh but in vain." Now the consciousness in which the Light of Truth begins to shine again after an attack of fear or unhappiness, is a city purified by that holy river, and it becomes a glad city, a city of God or good, a holy place for the tabernacles of the Most High. God is indeed in the midst of such a city, and when God, which is to say, our realization of God, is in the midst of our consciousness, then truly we shall not be moved.

God is in the midst of her; she shall not be moved: God shall help her, and that right early. Here the Psalmist adds one of those simple touches, expressed in the most direct and childlike language, that go straight to the heart. He says "God shall help her—and that right early." This beautiful promise should remove the last traces of fear and doubt that may linger in the dark corners of the soul.

The metrical rhythm of the poem is preserved by a reiteration of the general theme in the next verse. *The heathen raged, the kingdoms were moved: he uttered his voice, the earth melted.* The heathen, needless to say, means your own wrong thoughts, those fears, doubts, self-reproaches, and shortcomings of every kind that come between you and your realization of God—the heathen forces that attack the holy city of your soul, sometimes lay siege to it for days and weeks, and sometimes even capture and occupy it for a time. Only for a time, however, if you hold steadfastly to God by constant prayer, for sooner or later, as surely as God lives, the kingdom of error shall be moved. He will "utter his voice" through your prayers and affirmations, and your salvation will come.

The third and last stanza of our treatment is an exercise of thanksgiving and praise. These Bible treatments are constructed with the utmost care and in the most scientific way. Usually, though not always, for there must be no hard and fast rules in prayer, they begin with an affirmation of faith in God. Then they analyze fear and worry, showing that God has no part in such things, and that we, therefore, need not fear them. They go on to remind us of the love and power and wisdom of God, and of our ability, as the children of God, to call upon His power in any kind of danger or trouble. They make these truths vivid to us with unexcelled literary skill, using the most diverse images and examples to that end; and then they commonly finish, as prayers nearly always should, with a song of praise and thanksgiving.

Now the Psalmist makes us say *The Lord of hosts is with us; the God of Jacob is our refuge.* This destroys the feeling of God being afar off. The "Lord of Hosts" is the title for God that stresses His great power and might. It is the *omnipotence* aspect of God, we should say technically. So here we declare that omnipotence is

with us, and working through us; and he carefully adds
that It is also the God of Jacob. Now Jacob stands for
the soul that is not yet redeemed, the soul still struggling in difficulty and conscious imperfection. Israel,
"the Prince of God," is the soul that has realized its
Divine nature; but Jacob is still in the midst of his troubles. So the Psalmist here reminds us that God is the
Great Power, the Lord of Hosts, for Jacob just as well
as for Israel.

*Come, behold the works of the Lord, what desolations he
hath made in the earth. He maketh wars to cease unto the
end of the earth; he breaketh the bow, and cutteth the spear in
sunder; he burneth the chariot in the fire.* Here he continues with thanksgiving, saying, in effect: Let us consider the power and the glory of this God who is always
with us; how His action in prayer transforms our conditions, and makes desolate, or destroys, our troubles
and worries; how He makes the wars—a splendid
name for that worrying and stewing in misery that
blights the lives of so many people—to cease in every
part of our consciousness; how He disarms all the
things of which we are afraid, not just putting them
out of the way for the time being, but absolutely de-
stroying any power they ever had. When you captured
an enemy regiment in those days, smashed their bows
and their spears, and burned their chariots, you had
put them out of action pretty completely. That regiment could never trouble you again.

*Be still, and know that I am God: I will be exalted among
the heathen, I will be exalted in the earth.* This really is
probably the most wonderful phrase in the whole Bible. It really is the whole Bible in a nutshell. "Be still,
and know that I am God." This is just the very last
thing that we want to do when we are worried or anx-

ious. The current of human thought that Paul calls the carnal mind is hurrying us along to its own ends, and it seems much easier to swim with it by accepting difficulties, by rehearsing grievances, by dwelling upon symptoms, than to draw resolutely away in thought from these things, and contemplate God, which is the one way out of trouble.

Train yourself to rise above this hurrying tide of error—error is always hurried; to sweep you off your feet is its master strategy—and, turning your back upon conditions, however bad they may seem, *be still, and know that I am God.*

Even in your prayers there is a time for vigorous treatment, and there is also a time to cease active work and, "having done all, to stand"—to *be still and know that I am God.*

This of course does not mean merely doing nothing, or going away to concern oneself with some secular thing such as reading a novel or a newspaper. It is being still *to know that God is God.* Such "stillness" is the reverse of laziness or inaction. The still dwelling upon God is the quietest but the most potent action of all.

The Lord of hosts is with us; the God of Jacob is our refuge. Here again metrical symmetry obliges the poet to close his wonderful poem with a repetition of the general theme. Spiritually, too, it is a most powerful and effective ending to our prayer. The God of power who helps weak and frail mortals in the day of trouble is working through us, and so all will be well.

Note: The word Selah is not part of the poem itself but a stage direction to the temple musicians who chanted the psalms as part of a liturgy.

To be afraid is to have more faith in evil
than in God.

1. The Lord is my light and my salvation; whom shall I fear? the Lord is the strength of my life; of whom shall I be afraid?

2. When the wicked, even mine enemies and my foes, came upon me to eat up my flesh, they stumbled and fell.

3. Though an host should encamp against me, my heart shall not fear: though war should rise against me, in this will I be confident.

4. One thing have I desired of the Lord, that will I seek after; that I may dwell in the house of the Lord all the days of my life, to behold the beauty of the Lord, and to enquire in his temple.

5. For in the time of trouble he shall hide me in his pavilion; in the secret of his tabernacle shall he hide me; he shall set me up upon a rock.

6. And now shall mine head be lifted up above mine enemies round about me: therefore will I offer in his tabernacle sacrifices of joy; I will sing, yea, I will sing praises unto the Lord.

7. Hear, O Lord, when I cry with my voice: have mercy also upon me, and answer me.

8. When thou saidst, Seek ye my face; my heart said unto thee, Thy face, Lord, will I seek.

9. Hide not thy face far from me; put not thy servant away in anger: thou hast been my help; leave me not, neither forsake me, O God of my salvation.

10. When my father and my mother forsake me, then the Lord will take me up.

11. Teach me thy way, O Lord, and lead me in a plain path, because of mine enemies.

12. Deliver me not over unto the will of mine enemies: for false witnesses are risen up against me, and such as breathe out cruelty.

13. I had fainted, unless I have believed to see the goodness of the Lord in the land of the living.

14. Wait on the Lord: be of good courage, and he shall strengthen thine heart: wait, I say, on the Lord.

Light and Salvation

T HE Twenty-seventh Psalm is one of the great treatments or meditations in the Bible. Treatment is a convenient technical term we use for Scientific Prayer, which is directed to the overcoming of a specific difficulty. When trouble of any kind comes into one's life it is because he has allowed his consciousness to fall to the level where fear and limitation can reach him. A treatment consists in working on one's consciousness to raise it to the spiritual level where the trouble, whatever it is, disappears. Any mental activity which enables us thus to raise the spiritual standard of the soul is a form of prayer, and the Bible abounds in such forms.

The history of a problem or a difficulty is often this: The student is worried about something, or he feels ill. As soon as he realizes what has happened he, owing to his knowledge of Truth, declines to accept the condition at its face value in the way that most people do; and he proceeds, in one way or another, perhaps with the help of a prayer such as this, to bring about the necessary raising of his thought. He reads the Psalm carefully, interprets it spiritually, allows his mind to dwell upon the principles enunciated, appropriates them to himself, and repudiates the negative suggestion, whatever it was, thus regaining his peace of mind. And when this has been accomplished the trouble is found to disappear.

The Lord is my light and my salvation; whom shall I fear? The Lord is the strength of my life; of whom shall I be afraid?

This one verse is a perfect little treatment in itself; indeed it is one of the most complete texts in the whole Bible. It is a text that might well be written up over the portals of every church and every school in the land, for within it is contained in embryo the complete Jesus Christ message. Consider what it says. It postulates not merely the existence of God, but the living Presence of God in man, for the Lord here means your own Indwelling Christ, the I AM. Then it goes on to state that God in you, the Inner Light, is no mere passive or static presence, but a dynamic power to do everything for you that you can possibly need to have done. Just consider what this one phrase promises—light, salvation, and strength.

You will find that these three words cover very completely everything that man needs, for they really mean understanding, power, and demonstration—and what more can you want than that?

To begin with light. "There is no darkness but ignorance," and in the last analysis all human weaknesses and tribulations are really but a lack of the Divine Light. "Light, more light," said the dying Goethe, and that has been the intuitive cry of humanity through all its history. But God is Light, the Bible tells us, and in Him is no darkness at all; and Jesus said, "I am the light of the world." If you look back over your own life, you will be certain to find that a great many of your troubles arose through no intentional fault of yours but through your ignorance or inexperience, or

through your want of realizing to the full the implication of some situation which you had to meet. In other
words, you suffered through want of light. Well, here
the Bible explains that the Divine Power in you will be
your light, and that you can train yourself to utilize it
as such at any time that you need it.

The Lord is the strength of my life. Having promised us
light, the Psalm now goes on to promise strength or
power. We are to have power to do whatever we need
to do, to meet whatever we need to meet, to tackle any
problem or difficulty that can present itself in our
lives. We are, in fact, to be "endued with power from
on high" and need no longer trust to our own inade-
quate efforts. God will show us at any time the meaning of anything that we require to understand, will
show us at any juncture what it is we ought to do, and
He will furnish us with Divine strength to do it.

This wonderful verse then sums up its great message in the word "salvation," which, of course, means
all-round harmony and demonstration; and with the
penetrating psychological skill so characteristic of the
Bible when it deals with the soul of man, it obliges us
to ask ourselves, point blank, what there is now to be
afraid of. And anyone who accepts the premises will
hardly have any trouble in reaching the conclusion
that there is nothing to be afraid of, because God lives
and reigns—and then the back of the trouble is already broken.

*When the wicked, even mine enemies and my foes, came
upon me to eat up my flesh, they stumbled and fell.* Of
course, "the wicked," and "mine enemies," as always
in the Bible, stand for our own thoughts, for our fears
and doubts of every kind; and truly indeed do they
sometimes come upon us as though "to eat up our

flesh"—most people have at some time or other been only too painfully conscious of the aptness of this telling simile—and here you are promised that they shall stumble and fall.

Though an host should encamp against me, my heart shall not fear: though war should rise against me, in this will I be confident.

Here the Psalmist reiterates his confidence and makes us, his readers, reiterate ours. He makes us say that our hearts shall not fear, and he makes us believe it too, and can you think of any more beautiful assurance in the world than just that one—"my heart shall not fear"? When you can say quietly and truthfully at any hour of the day or night "my heart shall not fear," the world has no more power over you—you are free. War of various kinds may rise up against you, but you will be confident, and therefore you will be victorious.

One thing have I desired of the Lord, that will I seek after; that I may dwell in the house of the Lord all the days of my life, to behold the beauty of the Lord, and to enquire in his temple.

For in the time of trouble he shall hide me in his pavilion: in the secret of his tabernacle shall he hide me; he shall set me up upon a rock.

These two verses constitute a remarkable expression of what is often called the second birth. Briefly this means that a man or woman has taken the most important step that a human being can take, that vital step in comparison with which all other experiences are of relatively minor importance. The new birth or second birth, or what you may be pleased to call it, means that you clearly understand and definitely accept the fact that nothing matters except attunement with God. When you can honestly say, "I realize now that nothing in life really matters except that I get my conscious attunement with God—because when I have that, everything else will rightly follow, and until I do get that nothing else can be right—and I am going to make everything else secondary to that," then you have really experienced the new birth whether the realization itself has yet arrived or not. When you have reached that stage you do not allow any external happening really to grieve you, or frighten you, or hurt you very deeply, because you know that external things are but passing shadows of no permanent importance. And now because they cannot bind you they cannot hurt you, and so you are free. And above all you do not allow the delaying of the realization itself to fret you to discourage you in the least because you know the Truth, even if you do not feel it.

This steadfast determination to dwell in the house of the Lord, to behold His beauty and to learn His secrets, means that you are set upon a rock and that your house of life is secure (see Matthew 7:24–27).

And now shall mine head be lifted up above mine enemies round about me: therefore will I offer in his tabernacle sacrifices of joy; I will sing, yea, I will sing praises unto the Lord.

This verse closes the first section of the treatment with a burst of that praise and thanksgiving that is so powerful for demonstration. Singing in the Bible is always the supreme expression of joy and exaltation, as we know. We note here that to "have your head lifted above your enemies" is not merely a graphic figure of victory but is an important metaphysical symbol. The head is the bodily expression for man's power of knowing Divine Truth—his Christ faculty we call it— and it is, of course, by an increase of understanding that we overcome limitation.

Hear, O Lord, when I cry with my voice: have mercy also upon me, and answer me.

When thou saidst, Seek ye my face; my heart said unto thee, Thy face, Lord, will I seek.

Hide not thy face far from me; put not thy servant away in anger: thou hast been my help; leave me not, neither forsake me, O God of my salvation.

When my father and my mother forsake me, then the Lord will take me up.

The Psalmist here employs the dramatic form of addressing God. This gives the prayer vividness and intensity; but he is really affirming that God does hear us when we "cry with our voice" or "speak the Word," as we would say. He goes on to claim in different ways that God answers prayer. The actual affirmative form is usually the most effective form for healing a definite condition; but do not hesitate to address God when you feel so inclined. Do not abandon *any* kind of prayer. In fact, do not give up anything in your religious life that you find to be helpful. This Christ Truth comes to us not to destroy but to fulfil; not to rob us of anything good, but to give us more and more of the All-Good.

Seek ye my face. Of course, this does not mean that God has a limited, material face like a man or woman. It is a well known symbol. It is true that in many of the great classical pictures, God is represented as a man—usually a man round about sixty years of age, and wearing a beard. But this was a well understood artistic convention. A man at that age was assumed to have attained the maximum degree of wisdom, and so it was really a symbolical way of expressing Divine Wisdom. The face, in fact, symbolizes the power of recognition. In everyday life it is by the face that we recognize people, not usually by their hands or feet, for example, and to seek the face of God means to seek a recognition of God's Presence to the point of realization, so that we "know" Him by experiencing Him. When we find a difficulty in getting our spiritual contact, it is as though God had hidden His face. Of course, God never does that, but we allow a veil of selfishness, doubt, and fear to come between us and Him. People sometimes speak of the sun having "gone in" when they really mean that a cloud has come between the sun and them, but, of course, everyone knows that the sun is shining unchanged on the other side of the cloud.

The Psalmist now strongly affirms this fact that God cannot and will not "hide His face" from His children, and he drives his point home by saying that even if his father and mother were to desert him, God would not do so. In the Orient where the family link is so strong that it overrides all private and personal considerations, this is a very telling statement indeed.

In other words, this section of the treatment shows us that doubts and fears may assail the Psalmist in the midst of his prayer—as they assail us all at times—but that he meets and vanquishes them in the scientific way.

Teach me thy way, O Lord, and lead me in a plain path, because of mine enemies.

Deliver me not over unto the will of mine enemies; for false witnesses are risen up against me, and such as breathe out cruelty.

The Psalmist now prays for spiritual understanding and for peace of mind. The enemies, as always, are his own fears, and these fears take their rise in the fact that "false witnesses" rise up and confront him. And no one who has been through this experience will doubt the appropriateness of that telling phrase that our fears are things "such as breathe out cruelty." Verily, doubt and fear are the cruelest things that can come into the life of man.

I had fainted, unless I had believed to see the goodness of the Lord in the land of the living.

Wait on the Lord: be of good courage, and he shall strengthen thine heart: wait, I say, on the Lord.

Here, the Psalmist following up the rhythmical play and interplay of thought, characteristic of the Bible, once more makes it clear to his own mind that his reliance is indeed entirely upon the Divine Power, and not upon his own limited resources, his intellect, or his will power, for instance. He says that unless he had believed God would perform the necessary miracle, he would not have expected it to happen at all.

The closing phrase is a powerful exhortation to be active and steadfast in prayer—that you ought always to pray and not to faint. To "wait upon the Lord" does not in the least mean neglecting a problem in the hope that God will come along and solve it for you. It means intensifying spiritual activity. Waiting on the Lord means praying constantly and systematically about your problem. The effect of this will be to "strengthen your heart," which means that you will receive encouragement and power to continue your prayers; and that your consciousness will be gradually changed until your problem melts away altogether in the realization of restored harmony and peace. Thus does God answer prayer.

1. The earth is the Lord's, and the fulness thereof; the world, and they that dwell therein.

2. For he hath founded it upon the seas, and established it upon the floods.

3. Who shall ascend into the hill of the Lord? or who shall stand in his holy place?

4. He that hath clean hands, and a pure heart; who hath not lifted up his soul unto vanity, nor sworn deceitfully.

5. He shall receive the blessing from the Lord, and righteousness from the God of his salvation.

6. This is the generation of them that seek him, that seek thy face, O Jacob. Selah.

7. Lift up your heads, O ye gates; and be ye lift up, ye everlasting doors; and the King of glory shall come in.

8. Who is this King of glory? The Lord strong and mighty, the Lord mighty in battle.

9. Lift up your heads, O ye gates; even lift them up, ye everlasting doors; and the King of glory shall come in.

10. Who is this King of glory? The Lord of hosts, he is the King of glory. Selah.

The Everlasting Gates

PSALM 24

ALL through the Bible we are taught that the demonstration of harmony, that is, health, prosperity, and happiness, is God's Will for man; because until he has attained all-round harmony, man is not expressing God—and to express God is his destiny.

The Twenty-fourth Psalm is the great summing up of the Bible teaching on this subject. In the unique Bible idiom it explains harmony, which is the true meaning of salvation; and it analyzes in a masterly fashion, as only the Bible can, the causes that produce harmony. In its literary form the Psalm is a magnificent prose-poem in five stanzas. The first verse constitutes a concise, and, at the same time, exhaustive statement of the great metaphysical law. Let us consider what it really says, or, in other words, let us translate the technical terms employed into the common phraseology of modern life.

The opening verse forms one of the best known phrases in the Scriptures.

The earth is the Lord's, and the fulness thereof; the world, and they that dwell therein.

These words are constantly quoted on all sorts of occasions, but the context in which they are used seldom

89

gives evidence of any spiritual understanding of their true import. At worst, I have seen them used as an attempt at consolation in the face of death or of great financial misfortune. The implication seems to be that as everything belongs to God, He is entitled to destroy whatever He pleases without consulting the feelings of mankind. At best, they are taken in the sense of pious, but rather vague, recognition of God as the general source of our supply. Of course, even the vaguest recognition of this primary fact is better than no recognition at all; but unless we get a definite, scientific understanding of the meaning underlying the words, we shall derive no real profit from them.

To suppose that God, the Great Source, Substance Itself, could cause, or even endorse death or misfortune, is the deadly error that lies at the root of all our troubles; and it is characteristic of the carnal mind thus to pervert a text which, above most others in the Bible, explains the real Law of Life and Prosperity. This carnal mind, as Paul calls it, is, of course, nothing but our own restricted and ignorant manner of thinking. To be ignorant of the laws of life, or to misunderstand them, cannot, it is true, change those laws; but it can and does cause us suffering and deprivation of every kind—even to the death-belief itself—until such habits of thought are corrected.

The key to the true meaning of this first stanza is found in the two pivotal words, "Lord" and "earth," and here at the very beginning we must pause and ask ourselves what we mean by the Lord. "God, of course," we will say, and that is true; but in the Bible the word "Lord," as a rule, means God in the special sense of our own Indwelling Christ; our own true identity, the Divine Spark—the I AM. So this verse states, once and for all, that the "earth" which, as we know, is a general term covering all our expression or manifestation, is under the jurisdiction of the I AM. Now all trouble of every kind really arises from the belief that the "earth" is subject to the dominion of some outer power or law which is able to govern it independently of the I AM, or to destroy it altogether. But the Law of Being is, that man is the image and likeness of God, and has full dominion over all his conditions—all of them—and our Psalm emphasizes this wonderful fact by adding *the world, and they that dwell therein.* Our earth, which is our world, down to every detail of our lives, is really under our own dominion, and is made and unmade by our word.

For he hath founded it upon the seas, and established it upon the floods.

Who shall ascend into the hill of the Lord? or who shall stand in his holy place?

He that hath clean hands, and a pure heart; who hath not lifted up his soul unto vanity, nor sworn deceitfully.

The hill of the Lord, or His holy place, means the realization of God. It is that vivid, real sense of the Presence, that wonderful experience of security and joy that is truly the peace that passeth all understanding. When one attains to this he knows indeed that all is well, and that nothing can by any means hurt him. At such times too he has a marvelous power of helping and healing others. This state of mind is really the one thing that is worth possessing, for having that, one has all; and lacking that, he has nothing. To reach this state is the real object of all our prayers and treatments. It is nothing less than the dominion that we are promised in Genesis; and here the Bible impresses this truth upon us, and also instructs us how we are to get it. It is indeed a "holy" place because nothing defiled in any way can reach us there. Sickness, poverty, and sin cannot enter; that is to say, we cannot feel that such things are real while we are in this state of mind, and, as soon as we feel that they are not real, they disappear into nothingness.

The inspired writer then goes on to tell us how we are to raise ourselves into this wonderful consciousness, and it is splendid to note that he makes a point of affirming that it is founded upon the seas, and established upon the floods. This means that people like ourselves with all sorts of limitations and difficulties are the very people for whom the promise is intended, and that in spite of all our shortcomings we may reach it too; for it is founded upon the waters— and water is always the human soul as we know it, subject, as we are only too sadly aware, to storms, floods, and sometimes even typhoons. So we see that there is not the slightest reason to be discouraged merely because one's present demonstration seems to be very poor and spiritual power seems entirely lacking. It does not matter, because the high consciousness is built upon just such stormy seas as this. "Many waters cannot quench Love, neither can the floods drown it." Having thus indicated, as the Bible does on almost every page, that God's salvation is for anybody and everybody, "the wayfaring man though a fool shall not err therein," it goes on in its usual practical way to explain exactly how the thing is to be done. It says that for the great task we require clean hands and a pure heart, and that we must not lift up our souls to vanity, nor swear deceitfully. These instructions are certainly definite, and it will pay us to study them in some detail.

First in logical order comes the need for a pure heart—"Blessed are the pure in heart—for *they shall see God.*" I suppose it is only life-long familiarity with this statement that blinds us to its staggering importance. Just try to realize for a moment the thing that is said here—*"they shall see God."* Think what that must mean, and think whether any price could be too much to pay for that experience—*to see God.* Well, the Bible promises that on certain terms the wayfaring man, you and I, may see God. Of course, you will understand that there is no question of "seeing God" with the physical eyes as one sees a man or a house. With the physical eyes one can see only physical things, and God is Spirit, and spiritual things have to be spiritually discerned. Also, spiritual perception is not a matter of apprehending outlines and surfaces as physical sight is. Spiritual perception is direct spiritual experience in which the subject and the percipient become one. Therefore, to see God means—as far as our restricted and crippled human speech can express the thing at all—a realization of perfect essential unity with Divine Goodness Itself.

But who are the pure in heart? In the Bible use of the term, the words "pure" and "purity" are not confined to physical purity, absolutely essential as that is; they are expanded to include freedom from every kind of error and limitation. Now all error arises from a belief in the possibility of a cause other than God, and so, fundamentally, purity means complete loyalty to the belief in one single, all-embracing, Omnipotent Cause, which is utterly good—God, Our Father which art in heaven. To believe in God as the only cause, and absolutely to reject any claim for a lesser cause of any kind; to refuse to concede the power of causation to such things as climate, germs, man-made medical laws, or laws of poverty or decay; to refuse to concede reality to the race limitations of time and space; and, in the face of appearances, to judge righteous judgment, and hold unswervingly to the One Cause—this is purity.

In the Bible, the heart usually stands for what we call the subconscious mind, and it is our subconscious mentality that we have to redeem and purify. To keep one's mentality consciously loyal to the One Power is only half the battle, though it is the first and therefore the more important half. The other half is to purify and re-educate the subconscious from the errors which have accumulated there in the course of time. If we do this work faithfully, we shall sooner or later arrive at the point where we really have a pure heart in the full Bible sense, and then we shall see God. Jesus had reached this stage when he said "the prince of this world cometh and findeth nothing in me," meaning that his subconsciousness was so purified that no limitation thoughts could have any effect upon him; although at one time he was "in all points tempted like as we are."

This purifying of the soul, not merely from the grosser sins which everybody recognizes, but from the thousand-and-one concessions to limitation belief that fill the everyday life of humanity, is the one and only pathway to freedom. It is a wonderful beginning when we accept the Spiritual Basis of the Allness of God; but it is only when we have begun to apply this truth in every practical detail of our lives, day after day—when we are not in the humor to do so as well as when we are—that we really begin to get results. This is to have "clean hands." The hand is always the power of manifestation of expression, and unless our expression—

our all-day thinking—is "clean," that is to say, spiritual and true, we have not clean hands, and we cannot expect to ascend that wondrous "hill of the Lord."

This wonderful lesson receives its emphasis by repetition in a slightly different form, as in the Hebrew literary tradition. So we are told that the redeemed, or saved, is he who does not give his soul unto vanity—another way of saying one who does not look for his happiness to manifestation instead of to Cause, or believe in more causes than the One. To swear deceitfully is to pin your faith to error, to have a real conviction, as so many people have, that evil is true.

He shall receive the blessing from the Lord, and righteousness from the God of his salvation.

This is the generation of them that seek him, that seek thy face, O Jacob. Selah.

To many it may seem that the purification of the heart, or the redemption of the subconscious, will be a long and wearisome task, but we have to remember that when we pray it is God who works and not we, and that tasks difficult or impossible to us present no difficulty to Him. If you will use the power of the Word to declare that God is purifying you, that God is setting you free, that God is inspiring and enlightening you, you will be amazed how seemingly impossible difficulties will be overcome; how old habits of thinking will fall away and new ones come in; and this is because you will receive your righteousness, or right thinking, from God. You have "sought His face," and, under the Great Law, you must begin to express something of His nature, for we always grow like unto that which we contemplate. Here the expression "O Jacob" means "O God of Jacob."

Lift up your heads, O ye gates; and be ye lift up, ye ever-lasting doors; and the King of glory shall come in.

Who is this King of glory? The Lord strong and mighty, the Lord mighty in battle.

Lift up your heads, O ye gates; even lift them up, ye ever-lasting doors; and the King of glory shall come in.

Who is this King of glory? The Lord of hosts, he is the King of glory. Selah.

This, the third stanza of the poem, is a glorious statement of the power of prayer. It is not exaggerating to say that it is probably the most glorious tribute to the power of prayer ever written. Gates and doors always symbolize understanding. A little thought will show the good logic of this. The gate or door is the place where we pass in or out of a city, in or out of a house, or a field, from one room to another, and so forth. In other words, it marks a change of consciousness. The *place* that you are in at any moment is really the state of consciousness which you have at the moment, and what we know as movement through space from one place to another, from Europe to America, or from the dining room into the drawing room, is really a partial change of consciousness. Of course, the only change of this kind which has any true value is the absolute change brought about by an increase in the understanding of Truth, and every time that we do gain such an increase we enter a fresh stage upon the Path. *Lift up your heads, O ye gates* is a dramatic way of telling us that it is only by the attainment of a higher degree of understanding that the *King of glory*—the vivid realization of God which we are seeking—can come to our souls. The gates and doors are told to lift up their heads, that is to say, to become loftier. In order that there may be no possible room for any misununderstanding of the mighty import of the message, we are then told to ask ourselves who the King of Glory is, and for what He stands; and it is impressed upon us that He is nothing less than the Lord, and that His is strong and mighty in battle. Not just a figurehead potentate, but a man of war, and the battle He fights, of course, is our battle for the overcoming of sin, sickness, and death.

The poet concludes with the re-affirmation that the power we contact in prayer is the Lord of Hosts, which is the Bible term for the aspect of God as Power.

These Bible Treatments are not mere literary exercises; they are definite methods for bringing about a change in consciousness. That means that it is of very little use merely to read one of them through hurriedly and then put it aside. A Treatment such as this Psalm should be read over slowly many times. As you read, you should pause frequently to become receptive for a moment in order to give a chance for inspiration to come through. Do not make these pauses too long. Pause for an instant, long or short, according to whether you are a slow or a quick thinker, and then, if nothing comes, continue reading.

Always, when reading the Bible, put in between the lines, so to speak, the thought that God is inspiring you. This is the way to get direct illumination on the Bible teaching, at first hand. Remember that other people's interpretations of the Bible, however helpful and stimulating they may be, can never be as valuable as those that you get for yourself. The Bible will give you new and wonderful knowledge having a direct bearing upon your own personal and private problems and difficulties, if only you will make that possible by adopting the right attitude of mind.

When your usual methods of treating a problem do not seem to be bringing results, it is a good plan to discontinue them altogether for a time, and to work exclusively for inspiration instead. This can be done by opening the Bible at random and reading whatever texts your eye falls upon. If the first page opened does not interest you, try elsewhere, and continue to do so until you do find something that gives you a new light. Note carefully, however, that it is a change in *consciousness* that you are now seeking, a change that will enable you to pray more freshly and effectively, and to be more sensitively receptive. You are not now seeking precise practical instructions. Do not take the working of any text literally as a direction for conduct, as such a practice easily ends in superstition. It is the letter of the Bible that killeth, the spirit that giveth light.

Daniel in the Lions' Den

DANIEL, 6

THE story of Daniel in the lions' den is one of the half dozen best-known stories in the Bible. I imagine there are very few people who have not heard it. It is a particular favorite with the children, and children are great judges of literary and dramatic power, as everyone knows who has ever tried to entertain one of them with a story. Now we learn from the Jesus Christ teaching that there is no such thing as chance. Everything happens in accordance with the law of cause and effect, and, therefore, when a story or a legend is found to have a world-wide circulation, and when that circulation continues generation after generation, we know that it must contain something of great importance to humanity. So it is with the story of Daniel's great demonstration. It contains within it a wonderful lesson in the Truth of Being, and for all these centuries it has helped and comforted millions of people, even though they did not have the scientific key to its meaning.

Let us now consider in a little detail some of the principal points of the story as it is given in the 6th Chapter of Daniel. We are told that Daniel was made what would be called nowadays Chancellor, or chief Secretary of State, under Darius. This was a position

99

of great honor and responsibility, but also one involving great personal danger to the holder. One could not
occupy such an office without making many powerful
enemies, and in that ancient Oriental world they were
apt to make short work of inconvenient officials in
high places, more particularly when the incumbent
was a foreigner. The sword or dagger, poison adminis-
tered in food, and even through wearing apparel such
as gloves or boots, were freely employed in such cases,
and, above all, political intrigue was used to bring the
obnoxious official to his end.

In the case of Daniel we are told that a carefully en-
gineered plot was carried through, which placed his
patron, Darius, in the position of being absolutely
helpless to save Daniel. Such plotters would take the
character of the monarch into account when laying
their plans. A small-minded, jealous man would be
handled in one way, a religious fanatic in another. Darius, who was neither of these things, but an intellectual formalist of a rigid type, was trapped in his own
weakness. Daniel was arrested, taken down to a pit of
lions, and thrown in. Such a pit of wild animals was
sure to be found near most Eastern palaces of those
days, the animals being required partly for display,
and partly, as in the present instance, to furnish terri-
fying examples of political punishment. Daniel, however, instead of being promptly torn to pieces, remained untouched, and in due course was liberated
from the lions' den without so much as a scratch.

Spiritually understood this is one of the greatest lessons in the Bible. Daniel is Everyman. The story of his
great tribulation is the story of any difficulty that can
come into your life, or into mine. Incidentally, it is the
story of the whole of your human experience in gener-

al, but it applies also to each individual difficulty that you have to overcome. Remember that every individual problem that you have to face is but a tiny model, as it were, of the great problem of overcoming our human belief in limitation, sickness, sin, and death, that is called in theology the Fall of Man.

When some great problem or trouble comes into your life you are, figuratively speaking, thrown into a pit of lions, and many fearful hearts have felt that this is indeed a very graphic description of the state of mind they have experienced.

Now let us look for the key to the story and we shall find it here in verse 10. *Daniel had acquired the habit of prayer.* Daniel was a man who practiced the Presence of God, not now and again, but constantly and regularly. This verse is very illuminating. We are told that Daniel knew that the warrant for his arrest was signed. (When you are working and praying regularly, along the right lines, you will always get to know anything which it is necessary that you should know; you will not be taken by surprise.) Daniel knew that trouble was pending, and immediately he started praying, or treating, about it. He did not pronounce an affirmation once or twice and expect it to work, like an incantation. He prayed, clearing up his consciousness, three times a day. *"His windows being open in his chamber toward Jerusalem."* Of course the "chamber" is the "secret place" of Jesus, or one's consciousness. Jerusalem is always the highest part of man's nature or personality, short of the actual realization of God; and so Daniel, three times a day, turned in thought to God and raised his thought as high as he possibly could. No one can do more than this. It is a mistake to think that you must get a wonderfully vivid realization of Spirit in order to over-

come any difficulty. Prayer will get you out of your difficulty whether you get any realization or not. You can
always open your window toward Jerusalem. Whether
you ascend Mount Zion, which is the realization of
God Himself, does not lie in your hands—the turning
toward Jerusalem does.

In the same verse it says *"as he did aforetime."* This
tells us that Daniel was in the habit of thus praying scientifically. Some people pray only when they are in
trouble, and then, naturally they do not find it easy to
get any sort of contact. One would not expect to practice on the piano only occasionally, and yet play well on
any desired occasion. Daniel made a regular practice
of prayer and meditation three times a day, and when
the dark hour came, this practice stood by him. He
knew beforehand that trouble was coming. He probably knew almost exactly what it would be. And he met
it by working steadily on his own consciousness in order to get rid of fear. He probably succeeded in doing
this even before his arrest, and was able to rejoice in
victory well before the victory itself made its
appearance.

Of course, the real causes of all our troubles lie
within ourselves. The only enemies we have to overcome in the long run are our own fears, doubts, selfishness, and so forth. These are typified by King
Darius and the plotters. All your enemies are within
yourself—*"a man's enemies shall be those of his own
household."* Darius represents, in particular, our belief in the power of the external world to limit or injure us. He represents none of the things that are
usually called evil, but rather our limiting belief in
the fixed and unchangeable character of outer things
that are in themselves good.

The truth is that no outer conditions have any power in themselves, no outer laws need bind us, when we appeal to the supreme Christ Law of Divine freedom and harmony; but we do not know, or we forget this great truth, and so we go on believing in and submitting to all kinds of supposed laws of limitation. We believe that we are too old to do something that we could very well do. We believe that a certain climate can adversely affect our bodies, when in truth it has no such power. I knew a man in London who was working for the municipal government, a service which is swathed in red tape and vexatious restrictions of every kind. Feeling this fact acutely, he remained in a subordinate position for three years through being under the impression that his qualifications did not admit him to a certain higher grade, the work of which he knew he could do very well. After these three years he learned accidentally that there was in fact no regulation such as he had supposed to prevent his holding such a position, and he promptly applied for it, and was appointed, with a considerable increase in salary. This is an example of a belief in an outer limitation which in reality could have been overcome at any moment. It is a good example of Darius. The supposed rule concerning qualifications was not, even supposedly, an evil thing like dishonesty, deceit, or murder, but a rule, good in intention, to insure the appointment of suitable people.

The plotters represent essentially evil things, such as the above mentioned sins, and of course Everyman has to reckon with these too. *"The law of the Medes and Persians, which altereth not,"* is a splendid expression of our usual notion of these outer limitations as being impossible to overcome, of there being things and conditions that we just have to "put up with."

There is a well-known picture of Daniel in the Lions' Den, which was certainly painted by an inspired artist. Most of my readers will know it, and I always keep a copy of it in my room. Daniel is shown *not looking at the lions,* but turning his back on them! What a lesson in Scientific Prayer or Treatment; what I have elsewhere called "the Golden Key." The more we think over any difficulty the more we amplify it, and staring at our lions causes them to grow and grow until they are as big as elephants. Daniel is shown looking upward toward the light—a graphic representation of the Practice of the Presence—and the lions, instead of looking ferocious or angry, seem good humored enough as they stroll about or stand watching him curiously.

Those who have had much to do with wild animals in their native jungle always insist that no wild animal will attack a man who is not afraid of it. In India many stories are told of true Yogis (that is those who follow the Rajah or royal Yoga which is the search for reunion with God, and not just the acquiring of the power to play tricks on the etheric plane) living among tigers and other beasts of prey in perfect safety, and the Bible itself tells us that a time will come when the lion shall lie down with the lamb, because man has gotten fear, and hatred, and jealousy, and condemnation out of his own heart, and has thereby changed the whole moral and spiritual climate of this planet.

When you are in trouble you are Daniel in the Lions' Den. The lions will seem terribly ferocious; but pray until fear has begun to go; keep knowing the Truth, in the face of all appearances; and you will come out of the lions' den safe and sound, without a single scratch, as Daniel did. Nay more—you will come out stronger and better for the ordeal, because no problem that we meet in the light of Truth ever leaves us where it found us. Every problem thus overcome is a definite step upward in the growth of the soul.

It is significant, is it not, that being unable to accuse Daniel of any of the ordinary transgressions, his enemies proved beyond a shadow of doubt that Daniel was a man who declined to worship (to believe in or trust) any power but GOD. In the sight of the world this was an indictable offense, but in the light of Truth it was shown to be Daniel's salvation.

The longer one continues in the Truth teaching the more convinced he becomes of the fact that this is a mental world, and that man's dominion lies within his own mentality. When once we have grasped this fact clearly and have determined to put it into operation in our lives, it seems as though our difficulties were over, and theoretically this could be the case. Practically, however, it calls for the most rigid and persistent watchfulness on our part, if we are not to be constantly straying from the true path of correct thought. "Watch and pray," said Jesus, knowing how subtle are the temptations to step aside into old errors. "The price of liberty is eternal vigilance," said an ancient sage, and never was this truer than in the life of the soul.

If you really want to demonstrate health, happiness, and true prosperity—and every student of Truth knows that it is his duty to demonstrate these things as soon as he possibly can—you must set aside a definite time every day for prayer and meditation, and for checking up upon your own daily conduct and demonstration, or want of demonstration. You must conduct the affairs of your soul in a businesslike way. Too many religious people fail to realize that the business of spiritual growth calls for order, method, and intelligent organization, just as much as does any commercial business or engineering enterprise, or any other important activity, if it is to be a success.*

So great is the power of prayer that not only will it get you out of any difficulty, but the things in yourself which produced that difficulty will be utterly destroyed forever, with all their associated thoughts and fears; and all consequences or collateral effects that might arise from the problem itself will be taken care of too—"*and brake all their bones in pieces or ever they came at the bottom of the den.*"

There is no end to a prayer. It echoes on forever in your soul. Long after the visible demonstration has been made and forgotten, the prayer that produced it continues to work for your spiritual advancement, for the creative power of a God thought is unlimited and eternal.

---

*The Fifteen Points should be studied on this subject (see page 272).

The Garden of Allah

ISAIAH, 35

There is no god but God. Koran

Thou shalt have no other gods before Me. Bible

EVEN those who love the Bible most are apt to make the mistake of looking upon it as merely a book, the greatest book ever written, no doubt, but still a book; whereas the truth about the Bible is that it is really a spiritual vortex in which spiritual power pours from the Absolute or Divine Plane into the physical plane or plane of manifestation.

But the Bible is not only the great source of spiritual truth, it is also the greatest collection of literary masterpieces that we possess. Almost every literary form is represented in the Bible, both in prose and poetry. History, biography, philosophy, the short story in its perfection—re-read some of the parables, for example—the epic, and even that supposedly modern form, the novel, are all found there. The Book of Job is really a play; and Revelation is a drama in form so strange and unprecedented that it remains in its entirety almost incomprehensible to most people, however much they may appreciate its separate details.

Above all, the Bible abounds in beautiful and powerful prayers or treatments, and this alone makes it for us the most important book in the world. This is because prayer is really the only thing that matters. The only way in which man can improve himself or his conditions, get a better knowledge of God—save his soul, in short—is by prayer. Prayer indeed is the only real action there is; that is to say, it is the only action that makes things different.

Whenever you pray, you change your soul for the better. If the prayer is very short or the degree of realization very poor, the change it brings about may be small, but it occurs. It could not by any chance happen under any circumstances that any man or woman could pray for a single moment without some result for good following. Whenever you pray, your whole subsequent life is, as a consequence, somewhat different from what it would have been had you not prayed.

Now prayer is the only thing that does change the *quality* of the soul. Any other activity may make a *quantitative* change in the soul by adding experience, or by extending one's fund of knowledge; but it does not change the quality. Only prayer does that, and it is the quality of one's soul that determines his destiny.

As long as there is no qualitative change in your soul, you will, under any given circumstances, say or do the thing that such a person as you are would say or do in such a case, because we never really act out of character. We are never other than ourselves. When we try to be other than ourselves by an effort of human will, we are just being ourselves all the more on that account. When you pray, however, you by that act become at least a slightly different man and, therefore, all your subsequent activities are different too. So prayer is that only thing that matters.

The word "treatment" is a technical term that many of us use for prayer that is directed to the overcoming of a specific, practical difficulty, and the Bible is full of prayers and treatments of every kind.

When you find yourself in any kind of trouble, no matter what it may be, whether you think it is caused by somebody else's conduct, or whether you feel that it is your own fault, or whether it seems to be no one's fault; in any case the only possible thing to do is to treat yourself about it. If you give yourself an efficient treatment—or it may be that several treatments will be necessary—then the difficulty, whatever it is, will presently disappear and you will find yourself out of your trouble. In other words, your prayer will be "answered," or, as we often say, you will make your demonstration.

But what is a treatment? Well, briefly, a treatment means that you recollect and realize the Truth about God until you have brought about a change in your own consciousness, whereupon, as a result of this change in yourself, the outer things completely change too. Note particularly that this does not mean merely that you gain courage or fortitude to meet your difficulties in a new spirit. That would be better than nothing, but not much better. The tremendous fact is that prayer does change things. As a consequence of the change in your mentality that results from your treatment, outer conditions change completely. Other people change their conduct and their attitude toward you. Unpleasant things that would otherwise have happened do not happen, and good things that would not have happened had you not prayed, do happen—

brought about by prayer alone. *Prayer does change things.*

Now how is the necessary change in consciousness to be brought about? Or, in other words, how is a treatment made? Well the first thing to realize is that merely repeating a form of words is seldom any use at all. (That is better than nothing if you should be so frightened or worried that you cannot do anything more. In fact, to cling to a single phrase may be the only thing that can save you in a great emergency; but fortunately such an extreme condition is very exceptional.) It is the change in feeling and conviction that matters. Any means that brings this about—and whatever means does it most quickly—is the best treatment. Whatever will raise your consciousness from the lower level of trouble to the higher level of freedom is a treatment. In many cases the quiet, thoughtful repetition of certain affirmations of Truth is sufficient, such as: "I am surrounded by the Love and Peace of God"; or "Divine Intelligence opens my way." Sometimes, and especially if you are faithful in daily prayer and meditation, the mere momentary "feeling out" for God will clear the most formidable difficulty with lightening-like rapidity; feeling out in thought, that is to say, without formulating any words at all. The reading of a page of any spiritual book that appeals to you or, above all, a few verses or a chapter from the Bible often constitutes a most powerful treatment. It is for this reason that the Bible has so many prayers and treatments included in its pages.

The literary arrangement in which we have received our Bible is very misleading in many instances. The divisions into chapters and verses was made comparatively recently. The original writers had nothing whatever to do with it, and it was done in an arbitrary fashion that paid very little attention to the subject matter concerned. So it happens that with a writer, such as Isaiah, for instance, his works have been run together with little or no regard to sequence of subject or chronological order, and then, so to speak, chopped up into approximately equal lengths which are called chapters. In addition to this, a great deal of material, splendid in itself but not belonging to the prophet called Isaiah, has been included. Of course this makes no practical difference at all, as long as we know about it. The actual writer of anything in the Bible does not matter in the least, because the true author of it all is the Holy Spirit.

One of the greatest prayers or treatments ever written is included among the writings of Isaiah, and is known to us as Chapter 35. This chapter number, as we have seen, is purely an arbitrary designation. The chapter itself has nothing in particular to do with either Chapter 34 or Chapter 36. That number has no more intrinsic significance than the number a book may bear on the shelf of a library. As this chapter constitutes a particularly beautiful and effective treatment for any purpose, we shall now consider it at some length.

The first thing we notice is that in its literary form it is a glorious poetic rhapsody. The writer, in contemplating the wonder and the love of God, rises to a white heat of spiritual exaltation. The leaden shoes of fear and doubt that glue man to the earth in his everyday life are cast aside, and he rises on the pinions of Divine Inspiration into the region where all his petty limitations and handicaps vanish in the splendor of the Divine Presence. For the time being he leaves behind him every small and mean thing that keeps a man from God, from joy and freedom. And as he has succeeded in enshrining this transcendent experience in words that still live and glow today with much of his own original Divine ecstasy, it becomes possible for us in using this prayer with spiritual understanding, to kindle our own torch from the same fire, and, if we can tune ourselves in with his note, to transcend also any particular difficulty or group of difficulties that may be oppressing us.

The wilderness and the solitary place shall be glad for them; and the desert shall rejoice, and blossom as the rose. The first thing that strikes us here is that the writer is, of course, as all Bible writers are, an Oriental, and therefore he will give his message in the language and idiom of the Orient. This is so obvious that it would be unnecessary to mention it did we not know how many European and American people down to the last generation were in the habit of taking every Oriental simile and flourish at its face value, and often trying to apply it with the utmost literalness to some condition of life in London, or Manchester, or Chicago.

He begins his prayer in the best possible way that a prayer can begin, by a splendid act of faith in God. Always begin your prayers with an act of faith. Remember that Jesus tells us that faith in the Love of God will literally move mountains. And so our Oriental Prophet starts with what is doubtless the greatest affirmation of faith in God of which an Oriental is capable. He looks to God and cries: *The wilderness and the solitary place shall be glad . . . and the desert shall rejoice and blossom as the rose.* Think of it; the Oriental desert to become a garden, to blossom as a rose, to be a center of prosperity and riches. Nothing in our human experience can seem on the face of it less probable than this. No human trouble could be more difficult than this problem of turning the desert into a smiling garden. But with God all things are possible, absolutely all things, anything; and so to Him the redemption of a desert wilderness is just as easy as anything else.

The Bible is predominantly the book of a desert people. Always as the great drama of the Bible story moves across the stage of time, we are conscious of the desert as the background against which it moves. Palestine, a narrow strip of land not much bigger than Wales, was hemmed in by a desert on three sides, and by the unfamiliar and to them unattractive sea on the fourth. Almost everything that came into Palestine came across a desert. Goods and merchandise made their slow way in the leisurely desert caravans. All visitors who came to that country came through the desert and arrived wearied and parched with its sand and dust; and any new ideas that might filter into the world of Palestine had to filter through the desert too, and would inevitably arrive, like the travelers themselves, bearing about them something of the same desert atmosphere. For, just as to people living in the British Isles the sea is always the background—it is the sea that has moulded their history, and conditions their everyday lives, even though they may live so far from the ocean that they have never seen it—so the people of Palestine though they might never venture into the wilderness itself, were shaped and governed from first to last by the eternal, unchanging desert, and the conditions of life that spring from a desert home. Always the desert haunted them. There is not a page in the Bible in which we do not vaguely sense the eternal sands and hear the distant tinkle of the camel bells.

And so for us of the West it calls for a distant effort of the imagination truly to appreciate this splendid declaration with which the Poet opens his prayer. He takes the one condition above all others with which man had been totally unable to deal, much less to conquer—the desert; the one condition perhaps which would seem to him as an Oriental to be eternal and unchangeable, the one condition, we may say, that it would be utterly hopeless to think of changing: and he declares that the goodness and love of God shall completely conquer this. How complete and thorough that conquest is to be is signified by piling up, in the Eastern way, symbol upon symbol—*it shall rejoice and blossom as the rose*—one of the richest and most splendid of God's creations, calling for a special quality of soil and particular care in its culture.

It shall blossom abundantly, and rejoice even with joy and singing: the glory of Lebanon shall be given unto it, the excellency of Carmel and Sharon, they shall see the glory of the Lord, and the excellency of our God. On and on he goes in pursuit of his great theme. The glory of the desert redeemed is to be in proportion to its former barrenness. It shall rejoice with joy and singing. Glory of every kind shall be heaped upon it, the especial glory that the Poet knew in his time as only to be found among the cedars of Lebanon; the austere grandeur that he felt only in Carmel; and the sweet, fragrant peace that he had known among the beautifully kept gardens of Sharon. He closes this first stanza, his opening declaration of faith, by reaffirming *They shall see the glory of the Lord, and the excellency of our God.*

In reading this carefully we begin to catch something of the Prophet's own Divine faith in the goodness of God, and as faith is infectious, we find the power of his understanding gradually fanning our tiny spark of it into a flame.

Below each level of thought in the Bible there always lies yet a deeper level for those who can find it, and so it is here. Lebanon, Carmel, and Sharon in detail stand for certain spiritual faculties in the soul of man that gradually develop as he persists along the pathway of spiritual awakening, and the Prophet here implies, for those who can understand, that these definite spiritual gifts are the outcome of such prayers as this. Of course, the desert or wilderness is a general term for any kind of trouble or difficulty. It may be a specific problem that you have to overcome, or, in the wider sense, the general state of feeling cut off from God, of which we are all so conscious to our sorrow.

It is interesting to note that, in a very wonderful and different sense, the desert may be taken to symbolize that state of mind in which man has attained to a high degree of concentration upon God. Sooner or later you will have to put God first in your life, that is to say, your own true spiritual development must become the only thing that really matters. It need not, perhaps had better not, be the only thing in your life, but it must be the first thing. When this happens you will find that you have got rid of a great deal of the unnecessary junk that most people carry about; mental junk, of course, although physical junk is very apt to follow upon this. You will find that you will do a great deal less running about after things that do not matter and only waste your time and energy, when once you have put God first. Your life will become simpler and quieter, but in the true sense, richer and infinitely more worth while.

This has usually happened in the desert. The true desert wanderer has few physical possessions, none of our artificial needs, and few of our so-called comforts; yet he is among the happiest of the human race. Commonly he fears nothing in life or in death. It was an Arab sitting at the door of his tent at night, free from the burden of useless possessions, his mind and heart clarified by simple living, who gazed up at the myriad golden stars so bright in the eastern sky; looked about him with uninterrupted gaze to the distant dusky horizon; and said, "The desert is the garden of Allah."

Strengthen ye the weak hands, and confirm the feeble knees. Say to them that are of a fearful heart, Be strong, fear not: behold, your God will come with vengeance, even God with a recompense; he will come and save you. The first stanza of this wonderful poem-prayer having led the reader to make a splendid declaration of faith, this, the second stanza, takes up definitely the task of working upon his consciousness direct. It says *strengthen ye the weak hands.* Here we meet one of the most important symbols to be found in the Bible—the hand. The hand, briefly, stands for the power of manifestation, or the capacity to express God's ideas on the physical plane. It is the power of getting things done. It is the power of making demonstrations, as we say, or of getting answers to prayer, and so the expression, *strengthen ye the weak hands,* is a command that we are to rise up out of limitation, refuse to put up with it, and insist upon harmony and freedom; that, in fact, we ought always to pray and not to faint. Jesus has told us by means of two separate parables that we are not to accept less than harmony; that we are to go on praying until we make our demonstration; that we are not to take "no" for an answer. And here the inspired writer teaches the same lesson. You should never "put up" with anything. You should never be content to accept less than harmony, peace, and freedom. Until you get these things you must be insistent in prayer.

This particular symbol is a very interesting one. Man is, in his true nature, a spiritual being, a spark from the Divine Fire, but this devine spark, the I AM, has to be embodied, and the human body with which we are familiar, which we all carry about with us, is really but an embodiment of the various faculties and capacities of the Divine I AM. Actually we are at present seeing this embodiment in a very, very limited way, even in the case of the most healthy and beautiful bodies; nevertheless that is what it is. The Real Self, or I AM, has the power of manifesting absolutely any idea or set of ideas which it can understand, even to some extent; and this power we see embodied as the hand. In all ages the hand has been understood symbolically in this way. We speak of a thing being handy. A person who performs all sorts of essential business for another is often spoken of as his "right hand." At banquets the guest of honor is placed at the right hand of the host. The Christ Truth "sitteth at the right hand of God, the Father Almighty"—it is the Christ nature that manifests God through man. The word for hand, in Latin, is *manus* and this is derived originally from a Sanskrit word meaning the thinker. Our English word "man" ultimately derives from the same root and carries the same implicit meaning. And we know that it is man's *raison d'être* to manifest God. Man the manifestor is or should be the hand of God through which God works, and this he is through his power of thought, because he is essentially a thinker. When we wish to paralyze a man's activities we handcuff him, thereby putting his hands out of action, and to have both hands amputated is reckoned as almost complete disablement.

Confirm the feeble knees. This is a very obvious figure for getting rid of fear. There are not many of the sons of men who have not at some time or other known what it was to feel their knees almost literally going from under them through nervousness or fear. Such a condition, unless overcome, is the prelude to the total collapse of the body in what we call a faint. Now when people are in grave difficulties and are beginning to lose their courage—and to lose courage is to lose all—the soul may very aptly be described as being in this condition. The Prophet therefore strikes boldly at our weak hands and feeble knees and proceeds to confirm them, or make them firm, by bringing to mind the truth about God. One might well say indeed that essentially Scientific Prayer or Treatment is just this thing of pausing to *recollect the truth about God.* We do not try to do something with our prayers in the sense of seeking to manipulate things to our liking. Such a proceeding would be will power and not prayer, but we pause in the current of material things and *recollect* what we know to be the truth about God. This acceptation and re-affirmation of the Truth is what brings a spiritual demonstration.

The Prophet says with unanswerable simplicity: *Behold, your God will come with vengeance, even God with a recompense; he will come and save you.* And why? Because you are saying your prayers. Because, instead of being carried away in the tide of difficulty as the "heathen" or non-pray-er is, you have paused to recollect the truth about God. You have made the magnificent declaration of faith in the first stanza, and so the action of

God will now come into your life with vengeance or vindication.

People sometimes wonder why a loving God should allow them to get into trouble at all in the first place, or why He does not help them without waiting for their prayers. The answer is that we have free will. This is the most precious of all things for us because it is our identity in God as the I AM. If God were to interfere in our lives without our having called upon Him through prayer, our free will would be abrogated, and we should lose our identity. Actually this could not happen, because it would be against the Law of Being. We have to know here that this word "vengeance" in the Bible is a technical term meaning *vindication*. Needless to say, God, Infinite Mind, is not capable of approaching anything like what is know among men as revenge. What happens is that the action of God following upon your prayer *vindicates* the Law of Being, and as this Law is the law of perfect good you are saved. The demonstration may figuratively be described as the recompense for your treatment.

Then the eyes of the blind shall be opened, and the ears of the deaf shall be unstopped. Then shall the lame man leap as an hart, and tongue of the dumb sing: for in the wilderness shall waters break out, and streams in the desert. These two phrases constitute one of the most wonderful passages in the whole Bible. There is no other that can quite be put beside it. It is a song of triumph, and joy, and liberation, probably the most glorious celebration of the power of God in prayer that ever was written. Think what it promises, what it announces to be the natural result of spiritual prayer: The eyes of the blind shall be opened, and the ears of the deaf shall be unstopped, the lame man shall leap as an hart, and the tongue of the dumb shall sing! Is this a sufficient manifesto of spiritual healing? Is anything of importance left out? Can we, in the face of this, declare that any physical condition is beyond the reach of prayer? Can we dare say or think any more that with God some things are possible, and some things are not? The blind, the deaf, the dumb, and the crippled are to be set free and restored to health by the power of God.

Physical healing is one of the most glorious manifestations of the Universal Christ. It is the Beautiful Gate of the Temple, but it is not everything. It is the spiritual gift that has been most emphasized in the metaphysical movement for two or three generations, but as Paul was careful to imply in his enumeration, it is only one gift. The healing of the body is essential, but the thing that really matters of course is the spiritual development of the soul. What is a physical healing but the outer evidence that a step in spiritual development has been taken; and the physical healings enumerated here fully and beautifully as they apply to the physical body, are still more important when raised to a higher level.

It is glorious that the physical eyes of the physically blind should be opened, but the physical eyes also symbolize man's power of spiritual perception; and the magnificent promise of these two verses particularly implies that the gift of spiritual perception is to be acquired by prayer; and that when we earnestly pray for it nothing can prevent our getting it.

It is glorious that the ears of the physically deaf should be unstopped; but hearing, on the higher level, stands for spiritual understanding, and it is ten times more important that spiritually obtuse people should obtain an understanding of the truth about God and about life.

It is glorious that the physically crippled should regain his strength so that, throwing away his crutches and straightening his back, he shall assume the birthright of healthy manhood and run and leap like a deer. But it is ten times more important that moral and spiritual cripples should succeed in surmounting their infirmities and rise up in the free exercise of spiritual faculty and prayer.

It is glorious that the physically dumb should acquire the power of the physical word to speak and sing; but the tongue stands also for man's spiritual dominion or power, and it is a thousand times more important for the spiritually dumb, those men and women who have no power of spiritual demonstration, to acquire the power of the Logos or Creative Word which is their Divine inheritance, and learn to use it with telling effect for themselves and others.

Never before or since has the importance of these things both physical and spiritual been brought home so convincingly to men's hearts as here. And by way of a final emphasis on these transcendent truths the Oriental Prophet repeats his supreme argument: *For in the wilderness shall waters break out, and streams in the desert. And the parched ground shall become a pool, and the thirsty land springs of water.* To the Oriental reader no claim for Divine Power could seem to outreach this.

As we have seen, the sandy desert is to him the one eternal and unchanging fact, and to say that it shall be plenteously filled with water is to include all promises. We need to remember that, in that Eastern land, water is considered the most precious of all substances; comparatively small quantities are often transported miles upon miles upon the backs of camels and mules, and in remote desert places a cup of water is literally worth its weight in gold—far more perhaps, for it may mean the difference between life and death. We in the West who seldom know a real shortage of water, whose climate is, if anything, a trifle too wet for comfort, have to use our imagination again in order that we may realize how powerful and telling this simile really is, and all that it conveys of the power, and majesty, and resources, and love of God.

In the habitation of dragons, where each lay, shall be grass with reeds and rushes. As the result of prayer, of the recollection of the Omnipresence of God, and the affirmation of faith in His goodness, we are to lose our fear; regain our power of manifesting harmony and peace; obtain our physical healing, no matter what the malady may have been; and, above all, we are to develop spiritual perception, spiritual understanding, the power of speaking the Word with effect, and to acquire the capacity to develop new spiritual faculties altogether, for which there are no words in ordinary language. (We are but lame men without these faculties.) And now the Prophet says significantly: *In the habitation of dragons, where each lay, shall be grass with reeds and rushes.* This is a very remarkable and significant statement. The writer of this wonderful treatment knew all there is to be known about human nature. Our psychological experts are just beginning to scratch the surface of this subject; nevertheless much good work has been done by what is called the new psychology, in spite of its manifest errors; and people are just beginning to realize the existence of those "dark unfathomed caves" of our nature that are nowadays called the subconscious mind. We are beginning to realize that a thought is not dead or powerless merely because we are not consciously thinking it; but that it has simply floated out of sight under the ice, as it were, carrying with it all the potentialities that it had for evil, and much more in addition, now that it is out of sight. We are beginning to understand that a thing is not destroyed because it is suppressed, but, on the contrary, just as compression increases tremendously the detonating power of an explosive, so thoughts and feelings, and especially feelings that for one reason or another we do not care to face frankly, acquire an incalculable access of power for evil when they are suppressed into the subconscious and become what we call complexes. Indeed, psychotherapeutics has proved that a very large share of all our temporal ills spring from these very things. Now, Isaiah knew all this, and his name for these complexes is *dragons,* and a very good name too. It would be difficult to find a better one. And here he promises that as a result of prayer the dragons shall be cleared out and destroyed, and the watery depths where each lay shall become a secure and peaceful mead—quiet with grass and reeds and rushes.

And an highway shall be there, and a way, and it shall be called The way of holiness. We now come to one of the transcendent revelations of the Bible. For sheer power and splendor this passage stands alone. The whole stanza is quite unmatched either in Scripture or elsewhere. The Prophet rises higher and higher on the inspirational tide that bears him onward as he envisions the complete salvation of mankind that shall be. His eye sweeps along the whole flood of spiritual evolution, right on to the uttermost bounds where the human and the Divine shall be merged in final Unity.

For the individual, too, it is the promise and the means for the triumphant journey back to God. It is the great manifesto of salvation, the complete statement of the way of escape from limitation, sin, sickness, and death.

And an highway shall be there, and a way, and it shall be called The way of holiness. This is a definite and, one may say, businesslike statement that there is to be a way out. It means that it is no longer to be necessary for man to put up with anything less than perfect harmony. It really means that resignation to anything less than peace, health, and harmony—so far from being a virtue—will be known as what it actually is, a breach of the Law of Being. Let us make no mistake about this. Now that this way has been opened, resignation to limitation and inharmony is nothing but a fine name for laziness and cowardice. The Prophet definitely says that there shall be a highway. Now what is a highway? It is not a public main road, accessible to everybody, which all those who observe the law use with equal right. No one has any authority to put a barrier on the highway, to fence it off to the exclusion of certain people, or to exercise any kind of proprietary rights whatever. That is what a highway is, and the Prophet here definitely says that the Path of freedom and salvation is to be a highway. No man, no organization, no rules and regulations of either the dead or the living, have any power or authority whatever to forbid anyone to enter that highway, or to make any terms upon which he shall enter it. No conditions of membership, no entrance fees or entrance ceremonials have any authority over the inspired word. It is public. It is open. It is free.

Having prophesied a highway, the writer then definitely states that it will be a Way. Now a "way," of course, is a technical term meaning a way back to the consciousness of the Real Presence of God. It is what we often call the Path. And we may pause for a moment here to realize the tremendous importance of the statement that the Path is a *highway*. Most religious movements, at any rate the older and greater ones, have taught of the Path and how to enter upon it. But always they treated it, not as a highway, but as a private road fenced in by themselves, to the gates of which they alone held the keys. The Bible, however, came to the world to break down this exclusiveness and to say that the Way is a highway. It is really impossible for the student to overstress the importance of this fact. Again and again and again throughout history the open highway has been given to the people for a short time, only to be closed up again, and before very long, and usually by the very people who had opened it. So grave are the dangers that attend organized religion, so powerful and so subtle are the evils resulting from the accumulation of much property (an evil which overtakes almost every well organized church sooner or later), that unless we keep this point constantly fresh in our minds, we may be in danger of repeating the old mistakes.

The Prophet goes on to say that the Way or the Path is the path of holiness. Now, of course, we need to understand that the Bible uses the word holiness in a very much wider and more far-reaching sense than the usual one. The word "holiness" really means wholeness, not just holiness of character, rare and wonderful as that is, but complete holiness of life. This includes perfect bodily health—no invalid is holy in the Bible sense, however spiritual he may be in other respects—it includes the idea of happiness or true peace of mind, of prosperity, which means freedom from nagging fears concerning the necessaries of life; in fact, holiness means all-round health, prosperity, and spiritual harmony. Actually the words whole, holy, wholesome, heal, and healing, all go back to the same Old English root, because they are but different aspects of the same thing.

This does not in the least detract from the transcendent importance of what is usually designated holiness, the thing to which a great modern Rationalist referred sadly when he said "Holiness, deepest of all words that defy definition."

The Prophet goes on to say of this glorious highway, *the unclean shall not pass over it.* Now exactly what does this mean? Too often it has been supposed to imply that the ordinary human being, full of faults and shortcomings, and, still more, one conscious of graver sin, has no chance upon that highway; that it is reserved for the saint and the spiritual hero—for those who are indeed clean. Yet nothing could possibly be farther from the truth. What point could there be in providing a highway for those who are already "saved"? Did not our Lord say, "The well need not a physician, but those who are sick." And indeed to suppose otherwise would be like saying that one should not use soap until his hands were clean. The fact is, you do not bring a clean heart to God that He may love you for it; you bring your unclean heart to Him in order that He may cleanse it. The real meaning of this magnificent statement, the real bearing of this whole glorious final stanza, is that the highway shall be provided for the average human being, the "wayfaring man," you and me who stand in need of purification and salvation. The "unclean" are those very thoughts and beliefs of limitation, sin, sickness, fear, doubt, and so forth, that are the only things keeping us out of the Kingdom of Heaven today. These are the unclean; and once we are upon that highway they have no more power to hinder our progress. Their power of keeping us back in the darkness is gone.

No longer need frail, weak human beings fear to approach the highway. *It shall be for those.*

The wayfaring men, though fools, shall not err therein. Having shown that no degree of weakness or guilt can keep a man off the Path, if he really wants to enter upon it, Isaiah here takes up the other point that no lack of intellectual power or intellectual training can exclude him either. No want of what is called cleverness, or what is generally called education, makes any difference here. The most brilliant academic career, and the simplest unlettered background, are equally unimportant, provided there is the right intention, reinforced by right application. As a matter of fact, intellectual brilliance and much secular knowledge have kept many people off of this Path because, under our modern system of education, these things are very apt to beget spiritual pride. On the other hand, a good sound intelligence, while not in the least a guarantee of spiritual power, is likely to be very helpful in spiritual development, because it enables the candidate to appreciate the need for thoroughness, faithfulness, and disinterestedness; and it leads him to check up his results in order to insure that he really is making progress as time goes on. It saves him from living in a fool's paradise by supposing that he is demonstrating when he is not. It enables him to distinguish between spiritual progress and mere emotional indulgence. The great point is that we do not have to bring knowledge or wisdom to the Path, but that it is the function of the Path to equip us with these things.

No lion shall be there, nor any ravenous beast shall go up thereon, it shall not be found there; but the redeemed shall walk there. Here the whole story is repeated in another form, in accordance with the Eastern poetical tradition, which drives home its points by means of variety of iteration. Once upon the Path, troubles and difficulties will indeed still come to us, for a time at least; but now they come up from the inside, so to say; they emerge from the depths of our own personality, because they have no business to be there, and are to be dealt with once and for all. No longer are they lions or ravenous beasts from which we need to be protected; but rather are they problems to be solved once and for all, that we may be free forever.

And now this wonderful poem finishes up with one of the supreme verses of the whole Bible. Having entered and walked the Path, learned the lessons, and won the crown of completed understanding, our limitations and our spectral fears—for spectres they are, that and nothing more—disappear forever; and the glory of the Union, the grand transformations, is completed. Old things are passed away and *the ransomed of the Lord return, and come to Zion with songs and everlasting joy upon their heads; they shall obtain joy and gladness, and sorrow and sighing shall flee away.* Did ever man write like this? The "ransomed of the Lord" are of course those who have realized, not merely believed, but realized their oneness with their own Indwelling Christ; realized that that Indwelling Christ is in reality and truth themselves, not near to, not belonging to, but identical with themselves. Such as they who really have demonstrated the I AM.

And they shall return and come to Zion. Zion is the direct realization of God. Jerusalem is the highest thing in the human consciousness less than the Divine contact, but Zion is the realization of God Himself. It is to this that the Souls Triumphant will come, and, says the poet, with songs and everlasting joy upon their heads. They are to come singing, he says, and this is significant, for a spontaneous song is our natural expression of the highest joy. The instinct of the human soul which has not been cramped by taboos and inhibitions is to burst into song when it feels happy and free; and so the Bible rightly uses the idea of singing to express utter and spontaneous joy. And note that it says "everlasting" joy, not joy that may fade away with the lapse of time or the coming of some unexpected cloud. This joy is to be the joy of God, that never can and never will wane when once we have found it. So precise and thorough is the Bible's expounding of the way of man's salvation that here it makes a point of putting the joy upon their heads. Now the human head symbolizes always the Christ understanding of Truth, as distinct from mere blind faith, or simple emotional groping; and so here we see that this Divine joy is to be the joy of perfect *understanding*, which is the only real guarantee of permanence.

Our poem terminates its glorious upward sweep with a final clinching assurance, much as one might comfort a doubting child, an assurance that all this is really true, saying in the simplest language: *Sorrow and sighing shall flee away.*

Thou hast made us for Thyself, and our hearts are restless until they repose in Thee. Augustine.

FOREWORD TO THE GOLDEN KEY

I have compressed this essay into a few pages. Had it been possible I would have reduced it to as many lines. It is not intended to be an instructional treatise, but a practical recipe for getting out of trouble. Study and research are well in their own time and place, but no amount of either will get you out of a concrete difficulty. Nothing but practical work in your own consciousness will do that. The mistake made by many people, when things go wrong, is to skim through book after book, without getting anywhere.

Read the Golden Key several times. DO exactly what it says, and if you are persistent enough you will overcome any difficulty.

The Golden Key

S CIENTIFIC PRAYER will enable you, sooner or later, to get yourself, or anyone else, out of any difficulty on the face of the earth. It is the Golden Key to harmony and happiness.

To those who have no acquaintance with the mightiest power in existence, this may appear to be a rash claim, but it needs only a fair trial to prove that, without a shadow of doubt, it is a just one. You need take no one's word for it, and you should not. Simply try it for yourself, and see.

God is omnipotent, and man is His image and likeness, and has dominion over all things. This is the inspired teaching, and it is intended to be taken literally, at its face value. Man means every man, and so the ability to draw on this power is not the special prerogative of the Mystic or the Saint, as is so often supposed, or even of the highly trained practitioner. Whoever you are, wherever you may be, the Golden Key to harmony is in your hand now. This is because in Scientific Prayer it is God who works, and not you, and so your particular limitations or weaknesses are of no account in the process. You are only the channel through which the Divine action takes place, and your treatment will really be just the getting of yourself out of the way. Beginners often get startling results at the first time of trying, for all that is absolutely essential is to have an open mind, and sufficient faith to try the experiment. Apart from that, you may hold any views on religion, or none.

As for the actual method of working, like all fundamental things, it is simplicity itself. All that you have to do is this: *Stop thinking about the difficulty, whatever it is, and think about God instead.* This is the complete rule, and if only you will do this, the trouble, whatever it is, will presently disappear. It makes no difference what kind of trouble it is. It may be a big thing or a little thing; it may concern health, finance, a law-suit, a quarrel, an accident, or anything else conceivable; but whatever it is, just stop thinking about it, and think of God instead—that is all you have to do.

The thing could not be simpler, could it? God Himself could scarcely have made it simpler, and yet it never fails to work when given a fair trial.

Do not try to form a picture of God, which is, of course, impossible. Work by rehearsing anything or everything that you know about God. God is Wisdom, Truth, inconceivable Love. God is present everywhere; has infinite power; knows everything; and so on. It matters not how well you may think you understand these things; go over them repeatedly.

But you must stop thinking of the trouble, whatever it is. The rule is to think about God, and if you are thinking about your difficulty you are not thinking about God. To be continually glancing over your shoulder, as it were, in order to see how matters are progressing, is fatal, because that is thinking of the trouble, and you must think of God, and of nothing else. Your object is to drive the thought of the difficulty right out of your consciousness, for a few moments at least, substituting for it the thought of God. This is the crux of the whole thing. If you can become so absorbed in this consideration of the spiritual world that you really forget for a while all about the trouble concerning which you began to pray, you will presently find that you are safely and comfortably out of your difficulty—that your demonstration is made.

In order to "Golden Key" a troublesome person or a difficult situation, think, "Now I am going to 'Golden Key' John, or Mary, or that threatened danger"; then proceed to drive all thought of John, or Mary, or the danger right out of your mind, replacing it by the thought of God.

By working in this way about a person, you are not seeking to influence his conduct in any way, except that you prevent him from injuring or annoying you, and you do him nothing but good. Thereafter he is certain to be in some degree a better, wiser, and more spiritual person, just because you have "Golden Keyed" him. A pending lawsuit or other difficulty would probably fade out harmlessly without coming to a crisis, justice being done to all parties concerned.

If you find that you can do this very quickly, you may repeat the operation several times a day with intervals between. Be sure, however, each time you have done it, that you drop all thought of the matter until the next time. This is important.

We have said that the Golden Key is simple, and so it is, but, of course, it is not always *easy* to turn. If you are very frightened or worried it may be difficult, at first, to get your thoughts away from material things. But by constantly repeating some statement of absolute Truth that appeals to you, such as *There is no power but God,* or *I am the child of God, filled and surrounded by the perfect peace of God,* or *God is Love,* or *God is guiding me now,* or, perhaps best and simplest of all, just *God is with me*—however mechanical or dead it may seem at first—you will soon find that the treatment has begun to "take," and that your mind is clearing. Do not struggle violently; be quiet but insistent. Each time that you find your attention wandering, just switch it straight back to God.

Do not try to think out in advance what the solution of your difficulty will probably turn out to be. This is technically called "outlining," and will only delay the demonstration. Leave the question of ways and means strictly to God. You want to get out of your difficulty—that is sufficient. You do your half, and God will never fail to do His.

Whosoever shall call upon the name of the Lord shall be saved.

Getting Results by Prayer

A GREAT deal of confusion seems to exist in many minds concerning the precise avenue through which the Divine Power is to be approached, and realization and harmony attained. So many schools of thought seem to be competing for the attention of the student; so busy is the printing press; so many new books and pamphlets are written; so many magazines come and go; that people have told me that they have felt quite in despair of ever discovering what it really is that they must do to be saved.

Sometimes it seems as though the story of Babel were repeating itself in the metaphysical movement—and yet we all know in our hearts that the true Gate is narrow and the real Way strait. One well-known Eastern teacher of great spiritual power has actually published a pamphlet from which it appears that the genuine criterion of authenticity is to have no Path at all. This is the *reductio ad absurdum* which pulls us up short and restores the light.

The truth, of course, is this, that the only solution of the problem is definitely to contact the Divine Power which dwells within your own soul; and, having consciously done that, to bring it to bear upon the various difficulties in your life, taking them in due order, that is, attacking the most urgent first. This is the right way of working, and it is the only way that can possibly help you, or your affairs, in the long run. The real remedy for every one of your difficulties is, as we are told on every page of the Bible, to find and *know* the Indwelling Presence. *Acquaint now thyself with Him and be at peace. In His Presence is fullness of joy. Behold, I am with you alway.*

This, then, is the task, and the only one—to find, and consciously know, your own Indwelling Lord.

You see now how the confusion disappears, melts away, and the perfect simplicity of the whole thing emerges once you realize this fact. From this it necessarily follows that all schools and churches; all teachers, under whatever name they may be called; all textbooks, magazines, pamphlets, and what-not; are but temporary expedients for enabling you to make this contact. In themselves they are of no importance except as a means to an end. The best mode of approach to Divine things for you is the one that happens to make it easiest for you to locate the Inner Light within yourself.

Such things as temperament, education, family tradition, and so on, will make one book, or one teacher, or one school, more useful than another; but never as anything more than the means to a certain end. That end is effective self-discovery. "Man know *thyself*—thy true self which is the Divine I AM. And so we see that the best "movement," the finest textbook, the greatest teacher, is just the one that happens best to fit the individual need. It is entirely a practical matter, and the only test that ever could or ever will be of any use, is the practical one of *judgment by results*. Of course, Jesus anticipated this difficulty, and met it, as he has met all our difficulties. He gave us the simple and perfect standard: *By their fruits ye shall know them.*

The great peril to true religion has always been the building up of vested interests in wealthy organizations, or in the exploitation by individuals of their own personalities. An organized church is always in danger of developing into an "industry" which has to provide a living for numerous officials. When this happens the rank and file are sure to be severely discouraged from seeking spiritual things for themselves at first hand. A tradition of "loyalty" to the organization is built up as a means of self protection. Not loyalty to Truth, or to your own soul, be it remarked, but to the ecclesiastical machine. Thus the means becomes an end in itself and spiritual power then fades out. Rash promises and vague claims take the place of real verifiable demonstrations.

In the case of leaders who exploit their own personalities, the student is discouraged from going elsewhere for enlightenment or help; and here again "loyalty" to something other than God is allowed to block the avenue of Truth, and therefore becomes antichrist. What is this but the jealousy of the petty tradesman who warns a doubtful customer of the danger he runs in going to the "shop next door."

Remember that you absolutely owe no loyalty whatever to anything or anyone but your own soul and to the furtherance of its spiritual development. Your most solemn duty is to make everything secondary to that. "To thine own self be true; and it must follow, as the night the day, thou canst not then be false to any man."—*Shakespeare*

The first step that the earnest student must take is to settle on a definite method of working, selecting whichever one seems to suit him best, and then giving it a fair trial. That means that you must acquire a definite method or system of spiritual treatment or Scientific Prayer. Merely reading books, making good resolutions, or talking plausibly about the thing will get you nowhere. *Get a definite method of working,* practice it conscientiously every day; and stick to one method long enough to give it a fair chance. You would not expect to play the violin after two or three attempts, or to drive a car without a little preliminary practice.

Having got your method, set to work definitely on some concrete problem in your own life, choosing preferably whichever is causing you the most trouble at the moment, or, better still, *whatever it is that you are most afraid of.* Work at it steadily; and if nothing has happened, if no improvement at all shows itself within, say, a couple of weeks at the outside, then try it on another problem. If you still get no result, then scrap that method and adopt a new one. Remember, *there is a way out;* that is as certain as the rising of the sun. The problem really is, not the getting rid of your difficulties, but the finding of your own best method for doing it.

If ill health is your difficulty, do not rest until you have brought about at least one bodily healing. There is no malady that has not been healed by someone at some time, and what others have done you can do, for God is Principle, and Principle changes not.

If poverty is the trouble, go to work on that, and clear it up once and for all. It can be done. It has been done. Others have done it, and you can.

If you are unhappy, dissatisifed with your lot, or your surroundings, above all, with yourself, set to work on that; refuse to take no for an answer; and insist upon the happiness and satisfaction that are yours by Divine right.

If your need is self-expression—artistic, literary, or otherwise—if your heart's desire is to attain to eminence in a profession, or some kind of public career, that, too, approached in the right spirit, is a legitimate and worthy object, and the right method of Scientific Prayer will bring you the prize.

Keep a record of your results, and on no account be satisfied with anything less than success. Above all things, avoid the deadly error of making excuses. There are no excuses for failing to demonstrate. When you do not demonstrate, it never by any chance means anything except that you have not worked in the right way. Excuses are the true and veritable devil, who comes to tempt you to remain outside the Kingdom of Heaven, while the Gate stands open. Excuses, in fact, are the only enemy that you really need to fear.

Find the method that suits you; cultivate simplicity—simplicity and spontaneity are the secret of effective prayer—work away steadily; *keep your own counsel;* and *whatsoever ye shall ask in My name, that will I do.*

The Great Adventure

MANY people seem to have the impression that the sole object of metaphysical study is the overcoming of difficulties; but to suppose that, is to lose all sense of proportion. The Truth is to be sought for its own sake. The knowledge of Truth is its own reward, and that reward is health, harmony, and prosperity, to begin with; but this is only the beginning. The real object of the seeker should be the development of his own higher faculties and powers; in a word, his Spiritual Evolution.

Now it so happens that as fast as one acquires spiritual understanding, his circumstances improve in every respect—his health, his temper, his happiness and his material surroundings rapidly and automatically change for the better. *Per contra,* a want of true understanding automatically and necessarily expresses itself in some sort of difficulty on the physical plane, culminating in sin, sickness, and death.

When people find themselves in any difficulty, should they have some glimmerings of spiritual truth, they realize, however dimly, that a way out is to be found along the path of spiritual enlightenment, and consequently they study books, consult friends in the movement, ask for treatment or guidance, or take whatever step appears to be appropriate at the moment. This is the natural and proper course to pursue, and, provided they understand what it is that they are doing, it is only a matter of time before their difficulties—their ill-health, their poverty, their trouble, whatever it is—must disappear. They are, in fact, seeking spiritual enlightenment; they are working for a change in consciousness; and one cannot seek for an improved consciousness without getting it, nor get it without making a demonstration.

Misunderstanding and disappointment arise when people mistake the teaching for some kind of elaborate conjuring trick. When a man supposes that by a wave of the hand, or the repetition of an incantation, his circumstances can be changed for the better without any corresponding change in his own mentality, he is doomed to disappointment. He has not come into Truth, and the Truth movement has nothing for him.

During the past few years a large number of people of all sorts have consulted me about their difficulties, and they easily divide themselves into those two groups. Some people, for instance, are in trouble owing to some very obvious defect in character, but are quite unwilling to overcome this defect, or even, in many cases, to acknowledge it; they wish to continue in their mistake and to have prosperity or happiness as well. Needless to say, for them there is no relief until they have suffered a little more, and have been punished sufficiently to make them do what is necessary. The man who drinks, for example, is certain to ruin his business, and you cannot help him as long as he prefers whiskey to prosperity. Of course, if he is trying to give up whiskey, you can help him to do so, and then all will be well, but otherwise he will just have to go on suffering until his lesson is learned. Other people complain that they have no friends, cannot keep servants, and that they live unhappy, isolated lives; and a few minutes' conversation makes it obvious that there is an atrociously bad temper there which has driven everyone away. If such people are prepared to work to change themselves, the road is clear; but until they are, there is very little to be done for them.

Most of you who read this, however, will be seeking the Truth in the right way, and to seek the Truth in that spirit is really to have come into Truth. "You would not have sought Me had you not already found Me." That being so, you should not allow yourself to be worried or depressed merely because the demonstration is delayed. If you have sufficient understanding to believe in treatment, you have sufficient understanding to know that it must be only a matter of time before you are out of the wood—and what does it really matter whether it is a little sooner or a little later. Any delay in getting results can only be due to one of two things: Either the mental cause of your difficulty is very deeply seated in your consciousness and is requiring a good deal of work; or else you are not yet working in the best way, and if this is so, again it will be only a matter of time before you find what is the best way for you. In other words, once you are on the Path there is no hurry. "Oh, but," says someone, "in my case there is the most urgent hurry, because unless I make my demonstration by Saturday the verdict of the Court will be given against me," or "my creditors will foreclose," or "I shall lose the boat," or what-not. But the answer in Truth is still—*There is no hurry*, for the gates of hell shall never prevail. Let evil do its worst on Saturday; let the Court give its verdict; let the creditors strike their blow; let the boat sail. When Monday comes, prayer will still put everything right, if you can get your realization, and if not on Monday, then Wednesday, or Friday, or the week after next. Time does not really matter, for prayer is creative, and will build the New Jerusalem for you anywhere, at any time, irrespective of what may have happened, just as soon as you can get your realization of Truth, Omnipresent Good—Emanuel, which is God with you. This is the New Jerusalem which comes down out of heaven like a bride adorned for her husband, and is independent of any conditions of the physical plane.

When you are in difficulties, look upon the overcoming of them as a great adventure. Resist the temptation to be tragic, to give way to self-pity or discouragement; and approach the problems as though you were an explorer seeking a path through Darkest Africa, or an Edison working to overcome difficulties in connection with a new invention. You know that there is a way out of any difficulty whatever, no matter what it may be, through the changing of your own consciousness by prayer. You know that by thus raising your consciousness any conceivable form of good that you can desire will be yours; and you know that nobody else can by any means hinder you from doing this when you really want to do it—relatives, customers, employers, the government, bad times, so-called—nothing can hinder you from the rebuilding of your own consciousness—and this rebuilding is the Great Adventure.

You Must Be Born Again

W E ARE told concerning the teaching of Jesus that common people heard him gladly. This could easily have been inferred from the most superficial study of the Gospels. The "man in the street," unsophisticated by theology or philosophy, has an intuitive perception of fundamental Truth when he meets it, that is often lacking in highly trained minds. Intellectual attainments may easily beget spiritual pride, and this is the only sin upon which Our Lord was severe. Yet among the learned, too, there were those, the more spiritually minded, who felt themselves attracted to the new Teacher. He was unconventional, hopelessly out of favor with the ecclesiastical authorities, a flouter of hallowed traditions; and yet, deep calleth unto deep, and so he had his friends and followers in high places also. One of these who felt irresistibly drawn to seek for further light was Nicodemus. He had the thirst for Divine things that will not be denied, but moral courage was not his strong point, and so he sought out the Teacher by night. That he should have gone at all was proof of the compelling power of the urge. Clearly the unfoldment of his spiritual nature was, in spite of defects in character, the principal thing in his life, and clearly he was dissatisfied with the progress he was making. Jesus, he believed, had something to give that was vital, and that gift might be just the secret that had hitherto eluded him, just the key he needed to unlock the spiritual treasure-house of his soul. Jesus might be able to show him why he had so far failed to attain; why, as we should say in modern phraseology, he had failed to demonstrate. And the Master's explanation was simple, concise, almost overwhelming in its directness. He said: *"You must be born again."*

This statement sums up the whole science of demonstration as it is practiced on the spiritual basis. It is verily a textbook on metaphysics compressed into five words. It tells the whole story. You stand where you do today, wherever that is, because you are the man that you are. There is only one way under heaven by which you can be brought to stand anywhere else, and that is by becoming another man. The man you are cannot stand anywhere else; a different man cannot stand where you are now. If you wish to go up higher you can do so, and there is no limit to the height which you can attain upon that flight; but *you must be born again!*

Why is it that we make so little progress, compared, that is to say, with what we might and should make in view of the knowledge that we all, in this teaching, possess—at least in theory? Why do we not change day by day and week by week from glory to glory, until our friends can scarcely recognize us for the same men and women? Why should we not march about the world looking like gods, and feeling it: healing instantaneously all who come to us; reforming the sinner; setting the captives free; and generally "doing the works"? "Who did hinder you?"

And the reply is that demonstration, like all other things, has its price; that the price is that we be *born again,* and that in our secret hearts, too often, that is a price that we are not prepared to pay. We are in love with the present man, and all the things that constitute him, and we are not prepared to slay him that the other may be born.

We come into Truth with our little finger, and the great things will not come to us until we come in with the entire body; and there's the rub.

To come into Truth with your whole body is to bring every conscious thought and belief to the touchstone of Divine Intelligence and Divine Love. It is to reject every single thing, mental or physical, that does not square with that standard. It is to revise every opinion, every habit of thought, every policy, every branch of practical conduct, without any exception whatever.

This, of course, is something absolutely tremendous. It is no mere spring cleaning of the soul. It is nothing less than a wholesale tearing down and rebuilding of the entire house. Is it any wonder that all but the very strongest spirits shirk it. And yet, is it any wonder that without it one never really does get anywhere.

It means, as Paul said, "dying daily." It means parting with all the prejudices that you have inherited and acquired during all your life long. It means taking the knife to all the little faults of character, petty vanities, minor deceits, and all those lesser forms of selfishness and pride that crystallize your spiritual joints, and are so dear to you. It may mean giving up the biggest thing in your present life, but if it does—well, that is the price that must be paid, and that is all about it.

If you are not prepared to pay this price, well and good; but you must not expect to receive from the Law more than you pay for. A little finger in Truth is well, but it can only produce a little finger result. For a full-length demonstration the whole body must be full of light. *You must be born again.*

Dick Whittington

C HRISTMAS is the season of Panto-
mime, in London at any rate, and few
Christmases pass without the story of
Dick Whittington being told again at some theatre or
other. The children never tire of hearing the story of
little Dick and the chimes—and children as a rule are
good judges of Spiritual Truth. Although we shall
never be sure of the cold facts about the Sir Richard
Whittington who flourished at Guildhall so many
years ago, the Spiritual Truth about little Dick Whittington and what happened to him that evening on
Highgate Hill is eternal.

For the benefit of any who may not have heard the
story, it can be said that Dick Whittington was a little
boy who lived in Old London in the Middle Ages, that
he was an orphan, and quite friendless, and that he
was working in the scullery in the house of a wealthy
merchant of Cheapside. He was very cruelly treated,
however, by the other servants, and so at last, in des-
peration, he decided to run away. He had no one to
help or advise him, no one to whom he could look for
shelter or encouragement, and the place in which he
found himself having become intolerable, little Dick
did what so many other people do—he ran away from
his problem.

Of course, he had not the faintest notion where he was going to run to, or what he would do when he got there. He just felt that he must move at any cost, and so he ran away. This running away from one's problem is probably the most futile thing in the whole world, for the simple reason that all your problems are really in your own consciousness and, your consciousness being the essential You, it is not possible to run away from it. It does not make the slightest difference how fast you run, or how far you get; you will have to stop running some time, and when you do stop, there you will find your problems all lined up waiting for you. Having brought your consciousness—that is, yourself—along, you will naturally have brought your problems along too, unless and until you have solved them—in consciousness.

And so Dick started off, making a beeline away from Cheapside, and striking due north into the open fields, which he very soon reached, for all this happened a very long time ago. He followed a country road until presently he reached Highgate Hill, which he climbed. Beginning to feel tired by this time, he sat down near the top of the hill to rest. We are told that it was a beautiful summer evening, and presently as the sun began to set, the chimes of Bow Church came floating across the fields to where he sat. Bow Church stands in Cheapside, just near the house from which he was running away, and, after St. Paul's itself, it was, and perhaps is, the most important church in the City of London. If you are born within the sound of Bow Bells you are a genuine Cockney, but if not, not; so you will see how important it is. For Dick Whittington, however, the chimes of Bow Bells were to mean a very great deal more than that, for, in spite of all his troubles,

Dick had the spiritual faculty all but matured, and was ready to speak in the New Tongue (Mark 16:17).

"But how can it be," you may ask, "that anybody with a spiritual consciousness should be having difficulties? Are we not taught that health, happiness, and prosperity are the fruit of just this thing?" And this is an important point, and worthy of consideration. It is perfectly true that the possession of the spiritual faculty does guarantee, and is in fact the only possible guarantee, for all these things. But the spiritual faculty has to be recognized, realized, and brought out into manifestation. In its latent state it cannot demonstrate. It is proverbial that most people who do develop the spiritual consciousness through "coming into Truth," do so as a result of finding themselves in difficulties, or being down and out, to use the colloquial phrase, either physically, financially, morally, or otherwise. The reason for this is obvious once you have the key to it.

The children of this world are wiser in *their* generation than the Children of Light. Worldly, materially minded people—not necessarily evil people in any sense, but people without much spiritual development—are well adapted to worldly conditions, and, if they are reasonably sensible folk, they get on well enough with the world as it is. Those, however, who have developed *and brought into manifestation* the spiritual faculty are of another order. They are the Children of Light, and they can no longer live or move, or breathe freely in the pagan atmosphere of mammon. They are no longer under the lower law, but under Grace. And being under Grace, which is the Divine polity of God—gracious, and graceful too—all goes well, and all things are added as the needs arise.

But between these two states there is a transition stage, when the spiritual faculty has been developed, but is, so to say, still in the matrix of the soul—not yet born onto the plane of manifestation; and this is the stage where so much trouble appears. In this stage your spiritual faculty, the Wonder Child, is mature enough to have unfitted you for the atmosphere of the world, but it is not mature enough to take charge of and manage your affairs in the light of the Spirit. And now you are likely to have a bad time. Because you do not belong to the world, it will kick you about like a football, and the harder you struggle, the worse will things get. This, nevertheless, is the time to rejoice and lift up your heart, for now, if you are faithful, your salvation is·very nigh. These hard knocks are the indication that you are no longer in bondage to material law. The darkest hour is always just before the dawn.

As little Dick Whittington sat on Highgate Hill, the bells rang out the call to evening prayer. How many thousands of other people around London heard those chimes too, but found in them nothing out of the ordinary? How many tired and heavy laden men and women in the streets and alleys of the great city, or out in the fields and lanes adjoining, heard the very same sounds that summer evening as they floated over the roofs of the houses, and across the quiet English countryside; and yet received from them nothing to help them on their way? Dick, however, had the spiritual faculty well developed, although as yet he knew it not, and to him they spoke out clearly and unmistakably, pulling him up short, drawing the scales from his eyes, and showing him with instant clearness the next step he had to take. They said distinctly, startlingly, "Turn again, Whittington, thrice Lord Mayor of London." Dick was thunderstruck at this message, but at the same time so completely convinced that he never for a moment doubted what he had to do. He immediately retraced his steps; hurried back to Cheapside, and, so the story goes, not only faced up to the problem from which he had been running away, but solved it in the most complete and far-reaching manner. The Wonder Child was born.

It appears that he first demanded and obtained his rights in the kitchen, then graduated into the shop, gradually rose through a combination of inspiration and industry to be a partner in his master's firm, married the daughter of the house, became the leading merchant of the City of London, and, finally, as the bells had foretold, Lord Mayor.

It is interesting to note here that the old legend bears the hallmarks of its inspiration in detail. The step that Dick had to take was the last thing that he would have thought of doing on his own account. That is usually what happens when the Holy Spirit is guiding. When self-will whispers, the message is generally the kind of thing that we want to hear, the kind of thing that we have always approved of, the kind of thing that we should have done in any case. The Holy Spirit more often tells us to face right about and reverse our policy. Again we notice that, having received his guidance, there was no shadow of doubt or wavering in his mind. When you are doubtful or confused about a thought, it is probably not from God. When the Voice of the Lord speaks it is likely to be clear and unmistakable. It is by no means true that the thing you want to do is necessarily the wrong thing, but it may be. Some people have made a rule for themselves of thinking that the thing they want to do is probably wrong. This is a relic of the old theology. If you have been praying regularly, especially in the scientific way called Treatment, it is quite likely that the thing you wish to do is the right thing, but you have to make sure. The way to make sure is to go on praying until you get a really clear lead. When you feel confused or uncertain, pray for peace of mind. Usually it is better to take no steps as long as you are in doubt. Do not hurry; God never does.

If your guidance is not coming through, it is either because in your heart you do not really want it, having already made up your mind; or it is because you are too worried and tense to hear it. If the latter is the difficulty, claiming peace of mind will overcome it. When I treat for guidance, I always say: "The Holy Spirit is God, and God always finishes His Work, and delivers His messages satisfactorily; so my guidance must come through in a way that will be quite clear to me; and I say that it will." And it does.

The Yoga of Love

*Many waters cannot quench love, neither can the floods
drown it: if a man would give all the substance of his house
for love, it would utterly be contemned.*

ALL the old traditions tell us that there
is more than one path to the Great
Goal. Just as there is more than one
road up every great mountain, and yet all roads meet
at the top, so in the Spiritual Quest there are several
roads, all of which lead in due season to the One Great
End.

There is the path of knowledge. True knowledge of
Divine things is one of the appointed paths to attainment; but that path is by no means for everyone. And
there is the pathway of action—of organized activity,
perhaps one had better say—and the world needs this
too; but this again usually calls for a special gift, and
special circumstances in which to apply it. And there
are others.

The shortest and the easiest pathway of all is the
Pathway of Love. This really is the Royal Road to the
attainment of the Great Goal. It is the simplest of all
the paths, and it is the most direct and the easiest too.
And it is the one pathway which is open to all, everywhere, irrespective of what their personal conditions
or surrounding circumstances may be. For Everyman,

everywhere, the true Initiation, through the Yoga of Love, awaits every day.

In metaphysics we understand that Divine Love is the complete expression of all that is meant by the word Religion; that having that we have all, and lacking that, we have nothing. It, therefore, behooves us to have some little attention to the consideration of what we really mean when we talk about Love.

Of course, it goes without saying that we do not mean personal love. That is well in its own time and place, but it is not what we are considering here. In the Christian teaching, Love stands for something much bigger and finer and more powerful than any merely personal sentiment. Unfortunately, as with many other spiritual ideas, there is no word in the language which is perfectly appropriate to express it. Material language is made to fit material needs, and it simply will not satisfactorily express true spiritual ideas. For these we need the new Tongue of which Jesus spoke. We seldom realize, I think, how very much we really are in the hands of the dictionary. We think certain thoughts; we have certain experiences; and then language, with its hard and fast boundaries, says, "You shall not say that wonderful thing—you shall say only this"—and we find on paper the pale lifeless shadow of the thing that came to life in our soul.

So there is really no word in modern English to express the true Christian idea of Love. Our English Bible uses the word "Charity," and while no doubt this word fitted the need fairly well hundreds of years ago, it has since changed so much in connotation that there is now hardly a word in the dictionary more removed from the thing that we really wish to express.

"As cold as charity," has become a by-word. The very thought of charity—that is, of needing to receive charity—has alone led thousands of people to take their own lives sooner than have to contact the dreadful thing. And yet, in its true meaning it should convey just what we mean by Love.

Perhaps we can best approach the idea by saying that Christianity understands by Love the idea of universal good will, but plus something very much more than ordinary good will—that something which is nothing less than God, Himself.

Love is the motive power in Mind, and it is the quality of Love in Mind that leads it to seek for fuller and fuller expression, for Love always must be expressed. What we call Service, to use the term that has happily come into very general use of late, is really Love in action.

The principal aspects of God are: Life, Truth, and Love. These are the great Trinity in which Mind expresses itself, and we shall see now in what sense they are one and the same thing. Life is existence, and this is the Truth of Being. Naturally Life must have free expression, and Love is just this very thing, this perfect expression of Life. In other words, what we call Love is really the full and unrestricted expression of Divine Life itself. That is why it always means perfect peace, perfect holiness, perfect beauty, perfect joy— and why Jesus said, "I am come that they might have Life, and that they might have it more abundantly."

Now we see why the converse of Love is fear; and why fear is the supreme enemy of mankind. Everybody recognizes this fact today. All academic psychology is turning its attention to the overcoming of fear, and most schools of philosophy too now teach that fear is the thing that has to be rooted out. And fear turns out to be simply the absence of Love. "Fear hath torment but perfect Love casteth out fear."

The only reason we have any fear at all is because we do not love God enough. If we really loved God one-half as much as we love ourselves, of what should we be afraid? A great mystic said, "Love God—and do what you please," knowing that with the love of God in our hearts our expression could only be perfect; and a modern seer has told us, "You can get rid of any difficulty whatever from your life as soon as you can love God more than you love the error."

Anger, spite, resentment, and hate—all such things—are just so many alternative expressions of fear. Jealousy, malice, and "all uncharitableness" denote a belief that there is not enough good to go around and, therefore, if the other fellow gets all that he wants of good, we shall have to go short; and what is this but to constrict the expression of Life in one's own soul? If you tie a ligature very tightly around a human limb you know what happens; first it becomes paralyzed, and ultimately, if the process is kept going long enough, the limb withers away altogether.

Now, the absence of Love has exactly this effect upon the Soul. Condemnation, resentment, ill-will, are just so many constrictions upon the free flow of Life, and since they are allowed to exist, more or less, in so many human souls, is it any wonder that the world is filled with sin, sickness, and death?—that men and women grow old, and tired, and wrinkled, and worn, and ultimately lose their bodies altogether?—that the earth is desolated by wars, and famine, and pestilence?

Thus we begin to see the reason why the Jesus Christ teaching, under whatever name it may have been given out, has always laid so much stress upon the outstanding importance of Love. Unless we build up within our own souls a real and practical Love-consciousness, our other activities will be more or less futile. If we have the impersonal Love-consciousness sufficiently well developed toward all, everything else will follow. Indeed, many students have found that very remarkable things have followed upon even a few days' special work done on this subject. All sorts of personal difficulties simply vanish away after people have treated themselves a while for Love. As the months go along their faces sometimes alter in a remarkable way, for the body is almost the first thing to respond to freedom from fear and resentment. People have told me that they have felt twenty years roll off their shoulders, after treating themselves for a few days along these lines—and as they were *their* shoulders, they should know.

The more you learn of your religion, the more meetings you attend, and the more books you read, the more powerful becomes your thought, and the more sensitive your soul. You cannot afford today to hold wrong thoughts that would have mattered very little five years ago. You will be much more severely punished for every lapse now than you would have been in the beginning, and this is altogether well.

The Pathway of Love which is open to everyone in all circumstances, and upon which you may step at any moment—at this moment if you like—requires no formal introduction, has no entrance examination, and no conditions whatever. It calls for no expensive laboratory in which to work, because your own daily life, and your ordinary daily surroundings are your laboratory. It needs no reference library, no professional training, no external apparatus of any kind. All it does need is that you should begin steadfastly to expel from your mentality every thought of personal condemnation (you must condemn a wrong action, but not the actor), of resentment for old injuries, and of everything which is contrary to the law of Love. You must not allow yourself to hate—either person, or group, or nation, or anything whatever.

You must build up by faithful daily exercise the true Love-consciousness, and then all the rest of spiritual development will follow upon that. Love will heal you. Love will comfort you. Love will guide you. Love will illumine you. Love will redeem you from sin, sickness, and death, and lead you into the promised land, the place that is altogether lovely.

You may say to yourself definitely: "My mind is made up; I have measured the undertaking; I have counted the cost; and I am resolved to attain the Goal by the Yoga of Love. I can do this, and I will. Others may pursue knowledge to the farthest reaches of its wondrous growth; others again may organize great and marvelous enterprises for the benefit and uplifting of humanity; and still others may teach, and heal, and explore, or—if they feel the call—may scale the austere heights of asceticism; *but I have chosen the Yoga of Love.* Henceforth *my* field of work is right here in my own consciousness, and all my efforts and energies shall be directed to the cleansing and purifying of that from all that is not Love. Moment by moment, day by day, and week by week, I shall root out from my own heart, every atom of condemnation of my brother man, no matter who or where he may be, or what he may have done; every atom of resentment for any unkindness or injustice that has ever been shown to me, or to one that I love; every particle of jealousy of others, however cleverly it may be disguising itself; every smallest thought or feeling, in short, which is not an expression of Divine Love. My own heart is to be my workshop, my laboratory, my great enterprise and contribution to humanity."

This is the Yoga of Love, and while it requires no equipment beyond the readiness to practice it, yet that readiness is likely to cost so much in the way of effective self-sacrifice that those who truly seek it are comparatively few. It is not only the simplest, it is the greatest of all the paths, great in the magnitude of its individual results, and great in the work that it accomplishes for the whole race. To practice effectively the Yoga of Love is the guickest way to demonstrate over all your own difficulties, and because your mind is part of the race mind, it is actually the quickest and most far-reaching way in which you can elevate the race too.

It is the one path that is in practice open for every one to enter, at any moment. Here the isolated student is at no disadvantage as compared with him who can command efficient teaching. Here the poor man has perfect equality with the millionaire, and the dull has exactly the same advantages, no more and no less, as the intellectually brilliant.

The plain man earning a modest living in the factory or store can practice the Yoga of Love right there among the very surroundings in which he finds himself. The housekeeper at home, the sailor on the high seas, the farmer in his field, the nurse or the doctor in the ward, have all around them in their duties the perfect material for the Yoga of Love. The only question is whether one is really willing to pay the price—is really prepared to put God first.

Your Heart's Desire

A N OLD adage says: "God has a plan for every man, and He has one for you," and this is absolutely correct. Your real problem, therefore, in fact the only problem that you ever have, is to find your true place in life. Find that, and everything else will follow almost automatically. You will be perfectly happy; and upon happiness, health will follow. You will be really prosperous. You will have all the supply that you require to meet your needs, and this means that you will have perfect freedom; for poverty and freedom cannot go together. Until you find your true place in life, however, you never will be really happy, no matter how much money or distinction you may acquire; and until you are happy, you will be neither healthy nor free.

Whoever you are, God has not made you without definite purpose in view. The Universe is a universe; that is, it is a unified harmony, a Divine Scheme. There can, therefore, be no such thing as a misfit, or an unwanted or unneeded piece. It could not happen that God could create a spiritual entity such as you are, without having a special purpose in view, and this means that there is a special and particular place in it for you. God never repeats Himself, and so He has never made two people alike, and it is for this reason that no two people could ever do quite the same work, or express themselves in quite the same way. That is why, rightly understood, there really need be no competition. There need be no such thing as, say, two thousand people struggling for the same place in life. What the place may be, there can be only one person who can fill it perfectly; and there are one thousand, nine hundred and ninety-nine other places somewhere waiting for the other people if only they will find them.

But how is one to find his true place in life? Is there any means whereby you may discover what it really is that God wishes you to do? You may feel inclined to say: "Even if it be true that God has some splendid thing that He wishes me to do, and to be, how can I possibly find out what it is?" Perhaps you may even be tempted to add: "I am a very plain, everyday sort of person; my circumstances are extremely restricted; the conditions of my life are just drab commonplace. How then can there be something wonderful, beautiful, splendid awaiting me? Or, even if there were, how could I possibly get to know about it?" And the answer is Divinely simple—Already in your past life from time to time, God himself has whispered into your heart just that very wonderful thing, whatever it is, that He is wishing you to be, and to do, and to have. And that wonderful thing is nothing less than what is called *Your Heart's Desire*. Nothing less than that. The most secret, sacred wish that lies deep down at the bottom of your heart, the wonderful thing that you hardly dare to look at, or to think about—the thing that you would rather die than have anyone else know of, because it seems to be so far beyond anything that you are, or have at the present time, that you fear that you would be cruelly ridiculed if the mere thought of it were known—that is just the very thing that God is wishing you to do or to be for Him. And the birth of that marvelous wish in your soul—the dawning of that secret dream—was the Voice of God Himself telling you to arise and come up higher because He had need of you.

God is Infinite Mind, and that Mind is ever seeking for more and for new expression. "For such the Father seeketh to worship Him." Now, because you are a human being, you are intended to be a new point of expression for God—a focal point in Infinite Mind, in fact, somewhat as an electric lamp may be regarded as a focal point for the manifestation of the electric current in the circuit. A focal point for the Divine Self-expression—that is what you are intended to be; and if you are willing to become that, then you will be fulfilling your destiny, and you will experience absolutely perfect and unalloyed happiness and harmony, and eternal and unrestricted development. A few people have attained to this, but they are still comparatively few. The great majority have lives full of problems of one kind or another that they have yet to work out. If one has perfect bodily health—and how few have even this, really perfect health—then he probably has financial difficulties; or it may be family troubles, an unhappy home life. If health, finance, and home relations are satisfactory, there can still be a sense of frustration in other directions. In any case, in the absence of all-around fullness and harmony of expression, there is frustration; and frustration means trouble.

Modern psychology has been slowly realizing that many human ills are traceable to mental suppression, but our study of fundamental Truth teaches us that all trouble of every kind is really failure on the part of the individual to be a completely free focal point of expression for God.

You say that you are unhappy, dissatisfied, perhaps ill or impoverished, a failure; and this is simply another way of putting the fact that you are now allowing the Will of God to have free play in your life—*you are not doing the thing that he meant you to do.* You are drifting; or else you are trying to do something that He never intended you to do, and doing it badly, and distorting your soul in the process.

It is useless to blame Providence for your troubles, or to endeavor to saddle the responsibility upon other people. The universe operates strictly in accordance with Law, for God, among other things, is Principle, or Law, and where Law obtains there can be no room for the idea of blame. If you break a law, you suffer the consequences, and that is all there is about it. It is not a matter of blame or punishment. It is just an impersonal question of cause and effect. This may seem hard at first sight, but actually it is your certain guarantee of ultimate victory and freedom. Impersonal Law is certain to hurt you when you work against it, but, for the same reason, it is equally certain to help you and heal you when you work with it.

A human soul may be thought of as an opening through which Infinite Energy is seeking a creative outlet. If that outlet be a clear, open channel, all is well. If, on the other hand, it should become obstructed by any means, then the Infinite Energy, the Life Force, is frustrated, dammed back—and all sorts of local stresses are set up in that soul; and these we see as sickness, poverty, fear, anger, sin, and every kind of difficulty.

Now we are in a position to understand what the real art of living must be. It must be to make this channel clear, and to keep it clear; and if only we will do this, we shall find that health, prosperity, full self-expression—true happiness, in short—will then follow automatically.

People work so hard to *bring* health to their bodies; to *bring* prosperity, to *bring* happiness, to *bring* success into their lives; to *bring* artistic or literary gifts or talents within their grasp, to *bring* great new ideas from the outside; and, of course they continually fail, because we cannot "bring" a single one of these things from the without to the within. The actual development is just the very reverse—they have to be *released* from the within that they may appear on the without. In short, we have not to build on from the outside; our task, as Browning says, is "to set free the imprisoned splendor."

This process, the true manner of nature's working, is well illustrated by a simple anecdote. A certain man was working in his garden, assisted by his little girl. She had undertaken the interesting task of watering the lawn by means of the usual rubber hose. Matters proceeded harmoniously enough until she suddenly cried out in disappointment: "Daddy, the water has stopped." The father looked over, and taking the situation in at a glance, said quietly, "Well, take your foot off the hose." The child had inadvertently placed her foot and most of her weight upon the soft rubber pipe, and thus, by her own action, shut off the water that she needed. She, of course, removed her foot at once, whereupon the water again flowed freely.

Five minutes later, she once more cried plaintively: "Daddy, the water has stopped again." Her father glanced across and observed that now she had placed her other foot upon the hose. He replied: "Well, take your foot off." The child did so, and again the stream flowed freely, and, as she had by this time learned her lesson, she did not repeat the mistake, and completed the interesting task she had chosen, with much satisfaction to herself.

The ultimate cause of all our troubles is just this. Behind all secondary and proximate causes lies the same primary mistake. We have been acting like the little girl in the story; we have been pressing our feet and the whole weight of our mentality upon the pipe line of life, and then complaining bitterly because the water does not flow. Man's business is rightly to handle his Divine Spiritual Energy, and when he does this, he has found his true place, and then all goes well.

There is only one Fundamental Energy in the universe, but this energy may be applied by us either constructively or destructively, because God has given us Free Will. When we use it constructively, we are acting in harmony with the Will of God, and we are improving ourselves and our lives in every possible respect, and we are helping the world in general too. When we use it destructively, we damage ourselves, retard our progress, and waste an opportunity of helping mankind at large.

We use our energy destructively whenever we think or talk fear and limitation; whenever we grumble, or give way to self-pity, or indulge in useless regrets, or, in fact, in any form of negative thinking. Most of all do we use our God given energy destructively when we hold thoughts of criticism and condemnation of others. All bitterness, resentment, spiritual pride, and self-righteousness, are peculiarly disastrous methods of misusing the Great Power, and that is why such thinking causes the terrible havoc that it does in people's lives.

When we are in a condition of fear, anger, or worry, our Divine Energy, instead of flowing in some positive creative work, becomes dammed up within ourselves, like the water in the garden hose, and produces all sorts of trouble in soul and body. Meanwhile, our true work in life is either missed altogether, or, starved of the supply of Life Force which it should receive, it languishes accordingly, and we get mediocrity, poverty, and failure.

This is why all true spiritual leaders are so insistent upon the need for unselfishness in motive, for forgiveness of others, and of ourselves too, and for a general attitude of peace and good will toward all, for only in this way can we get that sense of true harmony and freedom that will permit the clear unobstructed flowing of the Divine Mind through us. Only in this way can we become a free channel for the Divine Energy to express Itself at the point of Being, which is our Selves. This spiritual state of consciousness in which the Life Force finds the unrestricted outlet which is so essential if we are to experience any kind of good, is technically known as *serenity*, and serenity, the great mystics are never tired of telling us, comes from within. It is not to be imposed from without by manipulating conditions or circumstances, or by any exercise of the will, but can only be derived from the natural, free flowing of our Divine Energy.

It is important to understand also that, for practical purposes, the amount of this Energy that one has at his command is limited, and, therefore, all that is frittered away in unnecessary or trifling activity or thought is so much taken out of one's capital, so much withdrawn from the things that really matter in life. If only people understood this, they would save themselves a great deal of wear and tear in the course of the day. And, if all waste is foolish, how much more deadly is it to *squander* one's resources upon the kind of thinking that is absolutely destructive. Yet, I have known people, as I suppose we all have, actually to rehearse trouble beforehand—thereby, of course, bringing it upon themselves—through saying such things as that they never had any luck, that they felt quite sure that some important scheme would fail, that they expected to be ill, and so on. One who understands the Law of Being and how it works would no more think of wasting thought by allowing himself to occupy his mind with inharmony than a business man would dream of throwing away money into the gutter as he walked along the streets.

As far as God is concerned, our supply of Divine Energy is, of course, absolutely unlimited; there is no check of any kind upon the amount of it that we can appropriate, or, therefore, upon the things that we can do or be. Yet, for practical purposes, it remains that any given time you can draw from the inexhaustible Source only in accordance with the measure of your understanding, just as you can draw water from the Atlantic only in accordance with the size of the vessel that you use. If you have a pint pitcher you can get only a pint of ocean water, although the number of pints in the Atlantic runs into inconceivable figures. At the same time, it is well to remember that very few people do, in fact, draw anything like as much of the Divine Energy as they could draw, even with their present understanding. Almost everyone is foolishly content to fill his pitcher, small as it may be, to somewhere very far short of the top.

It will now be clear to the student that discontent is not necessarily a bad thing. On the contrary, it is your duty to be discontented with anything less than complete harmony and happiness. Discontent is an evil only when it takes the form of discouragement, cynicism, or despair. A wholesome discontent with dullness, failure, and frustration is your incentive for overcoming such things. Without it, you would never find your true place. But, whoever you are, your true place is calling, calling; and, because you really are a spark of the Divine, you will never be content until you answer.

Remember that this call is the call of God, and when God calls you to His Service, He paid all the expenses in whatever kind of coin. "What soldier goeth to war at his own charge?" Whatever you may require to answer that call, God will provide. Money, opportunity, introductions, knowledge, training, freedom, leisure, strength, and courage—all will He furnish, if you be about His business and not your own.

Your Heart's Desire is the Voice of God, and that Voice must be obeyed sooner or later.

The Bogey Man under the Stairs

T HIS chapter is intended for people who are worried about something. I never tell people not to worry. To do that is to kick a man when he is down. Is it to be supposed that he is worrying for the fun of the thing, because it amuses him? If so, the malady would not be worry, and would call for different treatment. Of course there are people who grumble and whine because they like to do so. That is a bad condition to be in, and urgently needs attention, but it is not a case of worry.

No, worry is hell, and a hell from which the victim is only too delighted to escape when he sees the faintest shadow of a chance. Is it really possible to get rid of worry? That depends altogether on whether or not you understand the Truth of Being. If you do, the answer, is Yes.

Consider the following: A bogey that you do not believe in has no power to hurt or worry you. The Bogey Man who lives under the cellar stairs cannot frighten or deceive you *now*, because you do not believe in him; but when you were three years old it was very different. Then he had the power to raise your heartbeat to a gallop, draw all of the blood out of your cheeks, set your knees knocking together, and literally curdle the food in your little stomach. Given favorable conditions he could have stopped your heart altogether and killed you. Yet today he cannot cause one flicker of an eyelash—because you do not believe in him. That is the whole difference. Nothing in reality has changed. There is no Bogey Man there, and there never was one at any time; the difference is in you. You have now changed your thought. You have found that he was only a bogey, and so you are free.

Now it is exactly the same with any other kind of evil that may seem to be showing itself in your experience, for all evil is a bogey. It is there only because you believe in it, and it will disappear directly you cease to believe in it. The only "life" it has is what it receives from you. The only power it has over you is what you give it in belief.

Any material object or situation can be changed into something else by Spiritual Treatment or Scientific Prayer. No matter what the present state of any object, say an organ of the body, may be, it can be changed for the better by Scientific Prayer. No matter what may have taken place at some past time, it can now be changed into a different happening by Scientific Prayer. No matter what might happen tomorrow, without prayer, it can be made to happen quite differently by means of Scientific Prayer. Your sprained ankle, or the consequences to you of having ruined your frock with the ink-bottle, can be completely transformed by Scientific Prayer. Law week's law-suit, or next week's operation, and all possible consequences arising therefrom, can be completely wiped out of consciousness, everybody's consciousness; or they can be changed in character so that they are seen as a blessing for all concerned. It sometimes happens, for instance, that you buy some article, paying, perhaps what is for you a considerable sum of money for it, only to discover when you have got it home that you have changed your mind, and wish, too late, that you had not bought it. Never mind. Pray scientifically, and you will presently perceive that it was the right thing to get after all, and you will rejoice over the purchase, or in some other way you will obtain satisfaction concerning it. Of course, matters can only be changed for the better by Scientific Prayer.

Since these things are true, and they are, it becomes clear that the material plane cannot be "real" in the sense of being fixed or permanent; and once we grasp this fact it no longer has any power to hurt us. The truth is that our material conditions have no identity in themselves, being but the outpicturing of the convictions in our minds, and, as we always have the power to change our convictions, it follows that we can always change the outer picture too.

So your present trouble, whatever it is, is exactly like the Bogey Man under the cellar stairs. It is only a bogey, and the only power it possesses is the power you are giving it by believing in it. You must stop believing in it, and to do this it is only necessary to pray enough, or to get someone else to do it for you, and that unhappy picture will change, gradually or quickly, into something quite different from what it is now, or else disappear altogether.

With sufficient Scientific Prayer you can even make it vanish completely from memory, but that will probably not be necessary. You do not want to forget the Bogey Man under the stairs; you are quite indifferent about him because you really do know that he is only a myth.

Now you will see why it is possible to get rid of worry. When you can say confidently: *"Yes, at the moment this looks a bad business, but I know that by an active spiritual treatment I can change it into quite a different situation,"* real worry is at an end for you, and it is only a question of time before all-around health, happiness, and prosperity become the rule of your life.

"The name of the Lord is a strong tower; the righteous (Right Thinker) runneth into it and is safe."

No Results without Prayer

THERE is only one method of spiritual progress, and that is by the Practice of the Presence of God, whether we call this Scientific Prayer or Spiritual Treatment. There is no other way. Mankind is continually seeking to discover a short cut of some kind or other, because the carnal mind is constitutionally lazy; but as usual the lazy man takes the most pains in the long run, and having wasted his time in wandering up by-paths, he is ultimately driven by failure and suffering to the realization of the grand truth that *there is no substitute for prayer.*

This does not mean that any particular form of prayer is essential, but prayer there must be; that is, the conscious dwelling upon the Being of God. I have heard people say: "I did not treat when such a problem arose; I just knew the Truth about it, and the trouble disappeared." But this, of course, is exactly what Scientific Prayer or treatment is, and in its most beautiful and effective form. Such a person really means that he has not used some rigid or crystallized form of expression, which needless to say, is not in the least essential. Formal or set treatments are useful things to have by one, to fall back upon when spontaneity fails.

176

Then they help to focus the thought, and usually set the natural well a-bubbling. But—the thought's the thing—and the simpler and more spontaneous it is, and the more quickly it comes the better.

If your intuitive nature is well developed, you will seldom need to use formal statements at all. This is excellent—for who will trouble to climb a ladder when he is strong enough to leap over the wall? Unfortunately, however, there are a great many people with little or no intuitional development as yet, and many other people lose the ability to receive intuitional messages when worried or frightened. Then the ladder will probably be their salvation.

It must not be overlooked that very many people actually do all their work with formal statements of Truth, and get consistently good results by working in this way. Not through repeating affirmations like a parrot, it is needless to say. Those who work like a parrot inevitably make the parrot's demonstration— they remain in the cage. Of a good worker who used the same phrases many times it was said by a friend: "He constantly uses the old affirmations, but he stuffs them with fresh feeling every time." For one who has neither very much intuitional power at his command, nor yet the ability easily to express his thoughts in words, this is a model procedure. Meanwhile, in such a case the student must be particularly careful not to accept his want of intuitional power as a fixed thing, but to recognize it merely as a temporary disability to be gradually overcome. In fact, such a person should make a special point of treating himself for intuitional power regularly everyday—by claiming it, of course—*I have conscious Divine Intelligence. I individualize Omnis-*

cience. I have direct knowledge of Truth. I have perfect intuition. I have spiritual perception. I know.

Thus we see that practically all students of Truth do in fact employ treatment in one form or another, even though they may disclaim it. There are, however, a few people who actually refrain from all treatment on principle, but since one has never heard of their healing anyone, and they seem to be continually in personal difficulties of all sorts, the facts speak for themselves, and only go to prove the rule that treatment, or the Practice of the Presence of God, is the only road to harmony.

Faith

*Faith is the substance of things hoped for, the evidence of
things not seen.*
For by it the elders obtained a good report.
—HEBREWS 11:1–2

T HERE is a good deal of misconception
among students of Truth upon the
subject of Faith. Some of those who
are on the Spiritual Basis confuse the idea of Faith with
the conventional type of faith healing which always
fades into disrepute sooner or later because it cannot
be relied upon to give steady results. Nevertheless,
Faith, properly understood, is a necessary part of every demonstration.

The confusion arises because *blind* Faith is not really
Faith at all, but quite a different thing; namely, Hope.
Now Hope is not of the slightest use in demonstrations—frail, anemic, unfruitful in results, she it is who
maketh the heart sick. It is her elder sister, Faith, who
is the *substance*, the evidence, the sure and certain forerunner of victory. This is so because Faith properly understood is the result of the understanding of
Principle. When we have an adequate understanding
of the true nature of Being, we have Faith that the
Law, properly applied, cannot and will not fail us; and
so, when a practical problem presents itself, a call for

179

healing or supply, perhaps, a sound comprehension of this Law produces the scientific conviction, and then the demonstration necessarily follows. Thus it is the Elders, those in the possession of spiritual understanding, who receive that true report or demonstration.

The New Testament, among many other things, is a healer's case book, and in most of the instances cited, Faith was regarded as being a necessary preliminary— *"Stretch forth thy hand."* The essential doctrine on the subject is presented in the dramatic episode of the withering of the fig tree. The Master was desirous of proving to his students the power of understanding thought. For this reason he destroyed the fig tree. He naturally would not select an animal for this purpose, and a mineral would have been useless. A plant was the proper thing to experiment upon.

The following day the Disciples were amazed to discover that the tree against which the word had been spoken was destroyed. Upon calling his attention to this, he said in effect—"Yes, and that shows you the power of trained thought—you are surprised at this, but I tell you that you could order that mountain itself to be thrown into the sea, and it would happen, if you really believed it, and did not doubt in your hearts." Then he added significantly—"Before you practice the power of the word, if you are not at peace with everybody, treat yourself until you are."* This episode is so dramatic and so outstanding once we understand the nature of thought, that we are astonished that the world could have missed it so long.

The closing incident is particularly notable—he warned them of hostile or critical thoughts, *because of the harm they would do to themselves.* Many people are

*Matthew 21:19. Mark 11:12–14; 20–26.

greatly afraid of other people's thoughts, but there is
no need for any such fear.

Nothing can come into your experience unless it
first enters your mentality, and nothing can enter your
mentality unless it there finds something like itself to
which it can attach itself. As long as your heart is really
clear of ill-will, you are perfectly safe. On the other
hand, the use of the power of thought in hostility to
others could only result in very severe suffering and
punishment for yourself. According to your belief is it
done unto you. To think evil of Tom, Dick, or Harry, is
to think evil; and to think evil, *ipso facto*, is to call it
down upon yourself.

There are many who appreciate the power of Faith,
but lament that they do not possess it, and fear that because of this they can make no progress in Truth.
There is no need for such apprehension. The Will to
Faith in itself constitutes Faith, for the purpose of a
metaphysical act or treatment, and is sufficient. Disso-
ciate yourself from your own doubts. Remove your
consent, and they lose all power. You are not your
mind—you are not your thoughts—you are not your
doubts. Say: "Yes, my mind is full of doubts, but *I* am
not. I am not consenting to it—I have spoken the
word, and it shall not return void." This is the substance of the thing you hope for. It is the evidence of
the thing not seen. No power can hinder it.

The Seven Day
Mental Diet

T HE subject of diet is one of the foremost of the present day in public interest. Newspapers and magazines teem with articles on the subject. The counters of the bookshops are filled with volumes unfolding the mysteries of proteins, starches, vitamins, and so forth. Just now the whole world is food-conscious. Experts on the subject are saying that physically you become the thing that you eat—that your whole body is really composed of the food that you have eaten in the past. What you eat today, they say, will be in your blood stream after the lapse of so many hours, and it is your blood stream that builds all the tissues composing your body—and there you are.

Of course, no sensible person has any quarrel with all this. It is perfectly true, as far as it goes, and the only surprising thing is that it has taken the world so long to find it out; but in this pamphlet I am going to deal with the subject of dieting at a level that is infinitely more profound and far-reaching in its effects. I refer of course to *mental* dieting.

The most important of all factors in your life is the mental diet on which you live. It is the food which you furnish to your mind that determines the whole character of your life. It is the thoughts you allow yourself to think, the subjects that you allow your mind to dwell upon, which make you and your surroundings what they are. *As thy days, so shall thy strength be,* which, in modern language, may be translated *as thy thoughts so shall thy life be.* Everything in your life today—the state of your body, whether healthy or sick, the state of your fortune, whether prosperous or impoverished, the state of your home, whether happy or the reverse, the present condition of every phase of your life in fact—is entirely conditioned by the thoughts and feelings which you have entertained in the past, by the habitual tone of your past thinking. And the condition of your life tomorrow, and next week, and next year, will be entirely conditioned by the thoughts and feelings which you choose to entertain from now onward.

In other words, you choose your life, that is to say, you choose all the conditions of your life, when you choose the thoughts upon which you allow your mind to dwell. Thought is the real causative force in life, and there is no other. You cannot have one kind of mind and another kind of environment. This means that you cannot change your environment while leaving your mind unchanged, nor—and this is the supreme key to life and the reason for this pamphlet—can you change your mind without your environment changing too.

This then is the real key to life: if you change your mind your conditions must change too—your body must change, your daily work or other activities must change; your home must change; the color-tone of your whole life must change—for whether you be habitually happy and cheerful, or low-spirited and fearful, depends entirely on the quality of the mental food upon which you diet yourself.

Please be very clear about this. If you change your mind your conditions must change too. *We are transformed by the renewing of our minds.* So now you will see that your mental diet is really the most important thing in your whole life.

This may be called the Great Cosmic Law, and its truth is seen to be perfectly obvious when once it is clearly stated in this way. In fact, I do not know of any thoughtful person who denies its essential truth. The practical difficulty in applying it, however, arises from the fact that our thoughts are so close to us that it is difficult, without a little practice, to stand back as it were and look at them objectively.

Yet that is just what you must learn to do. You must train yourself to choose the subject of your thinking at any given time, and also to choose the emotional tone, or what we call the mood that colors it. Yes, you can choose your moods. Indeed, if you could not you would have no real control over your life at all. Moods habitually entertained produce the characteristic disposition of the person concerned, and it is his disposition that finally makes or mars a person's happiness.

You cannot be healthy; you cannot be happy; you cannot be prosperous; if you have a bad disposition. If you are sulky, or surly, or cynical, or depressed, or superior, or frightened half out of your wits, your life cannot possibly be worth living. Unless you are determined to cultivate a good disposition, you may as well give up all hope of getting anything worth while out of life, and it is kinder to tell you very plainly that this is the case.

If you are not determined to start in now and carefully select all day the kind of thoughts that you are going to think, you may as well give up all hope of shaping your life into the kind of thing that you want it to be, because this is the only way.

In short, if you want to make your life happy and worth while, which is what God wishes you to make it, you must begin immediately to train yourself in the habit of thought selection and thought control. This will be exceedingly difficult for the first few days, but if you persevere you will find that it will become rapidly easier, and it is actually the most interesting experiment that you could possibly make. In fact, this thought control is the most thrillingly interesting hobby that anyone could take up. You will be amazed at the interesting things that you will learn about yourself, and you will get results almost from the beginning.

Now many people knowing this truth, make sporadic efforts from time to time to control their thoughts, but the thought stream being so close, as I have pointed out, and the impacts from outside so constant and varied, they do not make very much progress. That is not the way to work. Your only chance is definitely to form a new habit of thought which will carry you through when you are preoccupied or off your guard as well as when you are consciously attending to the business. This new thought habit must be definitely acquired, and the foundation of it can be laid within a few days, and the way to do it is this:

Make up your mind to devote one week solely to the task of building a new habit of thought, and during that week let everything else in life be unimportant as compared with that. If you will do so, then that week will be the most significant week in your whole life. It will literally be the turning-point for you. If you will do so, it is safe to say that your whole life will change for the better. In fact, nothing can possibly remain the same. This does not simply mean that you will be able to face your present difficulties in a better spirit; it means that the difficulties will go. This is the scientific way to Alter Your Life, and being in accordance with the Great Law it cannot fail. Now do you realize that by working in this way you do not have to change conditions? What happens is that you apply the Law, and then the conditions change spontaneously. You cannot change conditions directly—you have often tried to do so and failed—but go on the SEVEN DAY MENTAL DIET and conditions must change for you.

This then is your prescription: For seven days you must not allow yourself to dwell for a single moment on any kind of negative thought. You must watch yourself for a whole week as a cat watches a mouse, and you must not under any pretense allow your mind to dwell on any thought that is not positive, constructive, optimistic, kind. This discipline will be so strenuous that you could not maintain it consciously for much more than a week, but I do not ask you to do so. A week will be enough, because by that time the habit of positive thinking will begin to be established. Some extraordinary changes for the better will have come into your life, encouraging you enormously, and then the future will take care of itself. The new way of life will be so attractive and so much easier than the old way that you will find your mentality aligning itself almost automatically.

But the seven days are going to be strenuous. I would not have you enter upon this without counting the cost. Mere physical fasting would be child's play in comparison, even if you have a very good appetite. The most exhausting form of army gymnastics, combined with thirty mile route-marches, would be mild in comparison with this undertaking. But it is only for one week in your life, and it will definitely alter everything for the better. For the rest of your life here, for all eternity, in fact, things will be utterly different and inconceivably better than if you had not carried through this undertaking.

Do not start it lightly. Think about it for a day or two before you begin. Then start in, and the grace of God go with you. You may start it any day in the week, and at any time in the day, first thing in the morning, or after breakfast, or after lunch, it does not matter, but once you do start you must go right through for the seven days. That is essential. The whole idea is to have seven days of unbroken mental discipline in order to get the mind definitely bent in a new direction once and for all.

If you make a false start, or even if you go on well for two or three days and then for any reason "fall off" the diet, the thing to do is to drop the scheme altogether for several days, and then to start again afresh. There must be no jumping on and off, as it were. You remember that Rip Van Winkle in the play would take a solemn vow of teetotalism, and then promptly accept a drink from the first neighbor who offered him one, saying calmly: "I won't count this one." Well, on the SEVEN DAY MENTAL DIET this sort of thing simply will not do. You must positively count every lapse, and whether you do or not, Nature will. Where there is a lapse you must go off the diet altogether and then start again.

Now, in order, if possible, to forestall difficulties, I will consider them in a little detail.

First of all, what do I mean by negative thinking? Well, a negative thought is any thought of failure, disappointment, or trouble; any thought of criticism, or spite, or jealousy, or condemnation of others, or self-condemnation; any thought of sickness or accident; or, in short, any kind of limitation or pessimistic thinking. Any thought that is not positive and constructive in character, whether it concerns you yourself or anyone else, is a negative thought. Do not bother too much about the question of classification, however; in practice you will never have any trouble in knowing whether a given thought is positive or negative. Even if your brain tries to deceive you, your heart will whisper the truth.

Second, you must be quite clear that what this scheme calls for is that you shall not *entertain*, or *dwell upon* negative things. Note this carefully. It is not the thoughts that come to you that matter, but only such of them as you choose to entertain and dwell upon. It does not matter what thoughts may come to you provided you do not entertain them. It is the entertaining or dwelling upon them that matters. Of course, many negative thoughts will come to you all day long. Some of them will just drift into your mind of their own accord seemingly, and these come to you out of the race mind. Other negative thoughts will be given to you by other people, either in conversation or by their conduct, or you will hear disagreeable news perhaps by letter or telephone, or you will see crimes and disasters announced in the newspaper headings. These things, however, do not matter as long as you do not entertain them. In fact, it is these very things that provide the discipline that is going to transform you during this epoch-making week. The thing to do is, directly the negative thought presents itself—turn it out. Turn away from the newspaper; turn out the thought of the unkind letter, or stupid remark, or what not. When the negative thought floats into your mind, immediately turn it out and think of something else. Best of all, think of God as explained in *The Golden Key*. A perfect analogy is furnished by the case of a man who is sitting by an open fire when a red hot cinder flies out and falls on his sleeve. If he knocks that cinder off at once, without a moment's delay to think about it, no harm is done. But if he allows it to rest on him for a single moment, under any pretense, the mischief is done, and it will be a troublesome task to repair that sleeve. So it is with a negative thought.

Now what of those negative thoughts and conditions which it is impossible to avoid at the point where you are today? What of the ordinary troubles that you will have to meet in the office or at home? The answer is, that such things will not affect your diet provided you do not accept them, by fearing them, by believing them, by being indignant or sad about them, or by giving them any power at all. Any negative condition that duty compels you to handle will not affect your diet. Go to the office, or meet the cares at home, without allowing them to affect you (*None of these things move me*), and all will be well. Suppose that you are lunching with a friend who talks negatively—Do not try to shut him up or otherwise snub him. Let him talk, but do not *accept* what he says, and your diet will not be affected. Suppose that on coming home you are greeted with a lot of negative conversation—Do not preach a sermon, but simply do not accept it. It is your mental consent, remember, that constitutes your diet. Suppose you witness an accident or an act of injustice let us say—instead of reacting by accepting the appearance and responding with pity or indignation, refuse to accept the appearance at its face value; do anything that you can to right matters, give it the right thought, and let it go at that. You will still be on the diet.

Of course, it will be very helpful if you can take steps to avoid meeting during this week anyone who seems particularly likely to arouse the devil in you. People who get on your nerves, or rub you up the wrong way, or bore you, are better avoided while you are on the diet; but if it is not possible to avoid them, then you must take a little extra discipline—that is all.

Suppose that you have a particularly trying ordeal before you next week—well, if you have enough spiritual understanding you will know how to meet that in the spiritual way; but, for our present purpose, I think I would wait and start the diet as soon as the ordeal is over. As I said before, do not take up the diet lightly, but think it over well first.

In closing, I want to tell you that people often find that the starting of this diet seems to stir up all sorts of difficulties. It seems as though everything begins to go wrong at once. This may be disconcerting, but it is really a good sign. It means that things are moving; and is not that the very object we have in view? Suppose your whole world seems to rock on its foundations. Hold on steadily, let it rock, and when the rocking is over, the picture will have reassembled itself into something much nearer to your heart's desire.

The above point is vitally important and rather subtle. Do you not see that the very dwelling upon these difficulties is in itself a negative thought which has probably thrown you off the diet? The remedy is not, of course, to deny that your world is rocking in appearance, but to refuse to take the appearance for the reality. (*Judge not according to appearances but judge righteous judgment.*)

Keep your thought positive, optimistic, and kindly while the outer picture is rocking. Keep it so in spite of any appearances, and a glorious victory is certain. Every side of your life will radically alter for the better.

A closing word of caution—Do not tell anyone else that you are on the diet, or that you intend to go on it. Keep this tremendous project strictly to yourself. Remember that your soul should be the Secret Place of the Most High. When you have come through the seven days successfully, and secured your demonstration, allow a reasonable time to elapse to establish the new mentality, and then tell the story to anyone else whom you think is likely to be helped by it.

And, finally, remember that nothing said or done by anyone else can possibly throw you off the diet. Only your own reaction to the other person's conduct can do that.

LIFE AFTER DEATH

RESURGAM

There is no death! Our stars go down
To rise upon some fairer shore;
And bright in heaven's jewelled crown
They shine for evermore.

There is no death! The dust we tread
Shall change beneath the summer showers
To golden grain or mellow fruit,
Or rainbow-tinted flowers.

The granite rocks in powder fall,
And feed the hungry moss they bear
The fairest leaves drink daily life
From out the viewless air.

There is no death! The leaves may fall,
The flowers may fade and pass away;
They only wait through wintry hours
The coming of the May.

And, ever near us, though unseen,
The fair immortal spirits tread;
For all the boundless universe
Is life; there are no dead!

Attributed to Bulwer Lytton

Life after Death

THERE is absolutely no reason to fear death. The same God is on the other side of the grave as on this side, and the Bible tells us that God is Love, and we know that He is also boundless Intelligence and Infinite Power. It is true that most people do fear death more or less, but this fear is partly that normal fear of the unknown that is apt to affect us all—the fear, as it were, of taking a leap in the dark—and partly it is the result of the false teaching on the subject that most people acquire in their youth. In the hope of disciplining them and frightening them into good conduct, people have been taught throughout the ages to regard death with horror.

Such, of course, is a mistaken policy, because good never comes out of evil, and fear in particular is never constructive. Nevertheless, men have been taught in most places and in all ages to fear death, in the hope that under the shadow of that fear they would behave themselves better during life.

The time has now come, however, when the mass of the people no longer believe in these threats but are prepared to hear the truth.

The actual truth is that there is no death. When a person seems to die, all that happens is that he leaves his body here and goes over onto the next plane, otherwise unchanged. He falls asleep here to wake up on the other side minus his physical body (which was probably more or less damaged) but enriched with the knowledge that he has not really died.

This is the story of what we call "death," and in most cases it is easier than being born.

To understand clearly how this process comes about, you have to realize that you really possess not one body but two. It may surprise you to be told that right here at the present moment you have not only the physical body that you know about—the thing that you see when you look into the glass—but a second body which is none the less substantial because you cannot see it, and that this body is made of ether. This statement may surprise you, but it is true. The etheric body is the same shape as your physical body, but it is slightly larger and it interpenetrates the physical body as air fills a sponge. It does not surround it but interpenetrates it. It may help you to think of it as a replica of the physical body in ether. There are a few people who can see the etheric body when they concentrate for that purpose, because they have the power of contacting much finer vibrations than can be perceived by the ordinary physical senses, but of course the vast majority lack this power.

All the time you are awake, your two bodies remain together interpenetrating each other, but when you fall asleep the greater part of your etheric slips out of the physical; and in reality this slipping out of the etheric is what constitutes sleep. The same sort of thing happens when you become unconscious either from taking an anesthetic or from a blow on the head, or if you fall into what is called a trance, or into some form of coma. All these conditions differ somewhat one from another, but they all have this in common, that more or less of the etheric slips out of the physical body taking consciousness with it.

The etheric body is not a simple homogeneous thing but is composed of several different ethers of different densities. Nevertheless, for our purpose we shall treat it as one. The physical body is composed of solids, liquids, and gases, and of many complicated and distinct organs, but in studying the biography of a man we treat his body as a unit, and in the same way we shall treat the etheric as one.

Now, it is this etheric body which is the repository of all your thoughts and feelings. It includes what are often called the conscious and the subconscious minds. It is the "psyche" of the psychologist, and it is in fact, your *human personality*. That is why personality survives death; because it resides in the etheric which passes over intact, and not in the physical which breaks up into decomposition when it is left alone.

I have said that your etheric is the seat of all feeling, and this is true. It may surprise you to hear that there is no sensation in the physical body, but such is the case. When you think you have a pain in your physical body, that pain is really in the etheric counterpart, and that is why anesthesia is possible. When you take a general anesthetic, the etheric is thrown out and therefore you do not experience bodily sensations. People undergoing a major operation under an anesthetic have sometimes remained perfectly conscious, but out of the body, and have watched the surgeon at work with interest and attention. When you take a local anesthetic such as novocaine, the local part of the etheric is driven out and you have no feeling there; but as the effect of the novocaine wears off, that portion of the etheric returns and, as those who have been in the hands of the dentist know, the pain gradually comes back.

In all these cases when the etheric leaves the physical body, it remains attached to it by an etheric ligament very much like a boy's kite floating at the end of the string which he holds in his hand. This etheric connection is called in the Bible the Silver Cord. It is bluish gray in color and is so elastic that the etheric body can go very long distances away and still remain attached to the physical corpus. In sleep, by far the greater part of the etheric slips out. In very materialistic and otherwise undeveloped people the etheric remains only a yard or two from the body, usually floating overhead; but with people of some degree of mental training, and especially with those who have some spiritual development, it passes right over onto the next plane, and sometimes beyond that. The difference between normal sleep, and anesthesia, and the different kinds of trance,* is a question of how much of the etheric goes out at that particular time—that is all. When we see people nodding asleep and then waking up and then nodding again, it means that the etheric is wabbling in and out. So your etheric slips out every time you go to sleep and returns when you wake up again— that is, as long as the Silver Cord remains unbroken.

Now, what is death? Well, death is the breaking of the Silver Cord. As long as that remains intact you are alive, whether you are conscious or not; but once it is broken you are dead. Death is the severing of the Sil-

*Numbers 24:4; Acts 10:10; Acts 11:5; Acts 22:17.

ver Cord. As soon as it is cut you are dead; you are definitely cut off from your physical body and your life on this plane is over.

So this, then, is death. Your etheric body, which is your personality, has severed its connection with the physical body, and as that body is your only means of functioning on the physical plane, you have finished with your earth life.

Now we come to the vital question: What precisely is it that happens to a person when he dies—when the Silver Cord is severed? What does he think? What does he feel? Well, as a rule, he immediately falls into a state of total unconsciousness which may last for days or even weeks. During this time the etheric (that is he himself) passes over onto the next plane, and he is in the next world. Here in due course he wakes up very much as we wake up from sleep on this plane, and his new life has begun.

It is an interesting fact that at the instant preceding death, the whole of the past life unfolds before the mind exactly like a moving picture reel flashing by. The actual speed is so great that it all happens in a split second Yet the mind sees every detail clearly. It is possible to come so near death that without actually dying one can still come back and continue to live after this has happened, but usually only in cases of near-death from asphyxiation. Only in near-drowning, suffocation, or gassing, as a rule, is the process slow enough to admit of this. This experience is really, of course, the unfolding of the subconscious mind, the "Judgment Books" of Scripture, and an exceedingly awe-inspiring and sometimes terrible experience it is, as one can easily imagine. It is with this authentic inside story of his life fresh in his memory, that the traveler begins his life on the other side.

Here, it is natural to ask: *Where is the next world situated?* Is it up in the sky? or down under the ground? The answer is that it is in neither of these places. The next world is actually all around us here. The so-called dead are carrying on their lives right here where we are now, but in their own world and in their own way. The reason we do not see them around us or collide with them is the same reason that one radio program does not interfere with another—they are on different wave lengths. There is not merely one etheric plane as many people think, but many, each one less dense than the previous one, going on to infinity; and they all interpenetrate one another. The activities of any one plane do not interfere in any way with those of any of the others for the reason just given. There is relatively a very great difference between the density of any one of these planes and that of the next one to it, so that normally there is no passing from one to another.

Upon waking up on the next plane, the "dead" person notes certain familiar aspects in the world about him, but remarks some curious differences too. If he has been very ill, or if he is an elderly person, he is agreeably surprised by a sense of well-being and youth. This is because, having left the worn-out body on the earth plane, it no longer restricts the full functioning of his mind. He is able to see his etheric body and it now seems to him as substantial as the old physical body seemed.

Again, one of the principal differences between this plane and the next is that there are four dimensions over there, whereas here, of course, we know only three. All objects there are four-dimensional, and it takes him some time to get used to that. Of course, a four-dimensional object cannot be described here in words, but you will easily see that it means an enormous extension of experience and therefore of interest. Consider how tremendously the world of a two-dimensional being—say a worm—would be expanded if he became three-dimensional, and you can realize something of the enhanced interest of the next plane when one of us goes over there.

Some writers unfortunately are in the habit of speaking of Heaven as the fourth dimension. This is quite wrong, because Heaven is a world of infinite dimension. What metaphysical writers say about Heaven is usually correct except that it is not the fourth dimension.

Also, there are new colors and new sounds on the next plane far surpassing in beauty the colors and the sounds which we have here, and it is a fact that new experience of every sort awaits the traveler on his arrival.

Perhaps the most startling change that the traveler has to meet is the fact that over there thought reading is the normal means of communication. In the next world thoughts are read directly, and therefore there is no deception. Everyone is seen to be just what he is, and there is no room for hypocrisy or pretense. All the labor and nervous strain of "keeping up appearances" that wears out the lives of so many foolish people over here is unknown there. You pass for what you are and that is the end of the matter. One soon gets accustomed to this, and then no one there would wish it to be otherwise.

There are no old people on the other side, for the following reason. What we see here as an elderly gentleman is in fact a man of mature mind whose body has begun to decay so that all his faculties are dimmed. He sees poorly, is almost deaf, moves about with difficulty, finds his memory impaired, and in many cases it is difficult to make him understand things we wish to say to him. These conditions are simply due to the decay of the physical body preventing his etheric from functioning efficiently, and now that the physical body is thrown away, he naturally regains the full use of his powers. And so, in the next world he will be a man in the prime of life. On the other hand, children who pass over, not having yet reached maturity of mind, continue to grow up on the other side until they too reach the prime of life.

There are many different localities on the next plane, differing very much one from another just as in this world we find countries as different as Sweden and Italy, for example, and even in the same city we find such different conditions as the squalid streets of slumland and the beautiful sections occupied by wealthy and cultured people. Indeed, there is a much greater variety of living conditions over there than anything that we find on this earth, so that one might compare the going over to the experience of a man who spends most of his life on a small island here, and then suddenly leaves that island to explore the whole world.

What is it that determines the kind of place to which you will go after death, and the sort of people among whom you will find yourself? Of course, it is not a matter of chance or luck any more than is the nature of your surroundings here. You will go to the sort of place, and be among the sort of people for whom you have prepared yourself by your habitual thinking and your mode of living while on this earth. No one "sends" you anywhere. You naturally gravitate to the place where you belong. You have built up a certain character, that is, a certain mentality, by your years of thinking, speaking, and acting on this plane. That is the kind of person you are at the moment, and you find yourself in conditions corresponding to your personality.

Remember that death makes positively no change in you; you are just the same person that you were before it happened. You have your full memory and you remember the general events of your life just as well, and often somewhat better, than you did toward the end of your life here. Students of metaphysics understand that all our conditions in this world are the result of our thoughts and convictions; and precisely the same thing is true of the next world. On this plane, people with the same interests tend to attract one another. The law that "birds of a feather flock together" holds throughout the universe.

There is, however, one extremely important difference—on the other side your thoughts are demonstrated *immediately*. In this world, as we know, it may take days, weeks, and even years, before mental states come out into manifestation, but over there they demonstrate at once. Whatever you think or feel strongly you experience instantly as an outer condition, and this is rather confusing at first.

To those on the other side, the ether seems just as solid as physical matter does to us, and in the beginning they expect it to have the inertia which it does not possess. They are surprised and disconcerted when they constantly find that it submits immediately to the moulding of their thought. They feel rather like a person whose automobile gets out of control and runs away with him. They think—and something happens to correspond. This surprises or frightens them, and

this fright causes an intensification of the phenom-
enon, or perhaps a seeming cataclysm; and "confusion
worse confounded" multiplies until the new comer
pulls himself together and learns to control his thinking. One would naturally suppose that under these
conditions he need only be very careful what he does
think, and all will be well; and this is perfectly true, but
in practice it is difficult instantly to change one's habits
of thought in this way. If we have accustomed ourselves when on earth to negative thinking—to
thoughts of fear, criticism, ill-will, or sickness—it takes
some time to overcome such habits when we get
across. Most of us know only too well (particularly
those of us who have tried *The Seven Day Mental Diet*)
that changing our current of thought is not an easy
matter; but, of course, it has to be done.

At this point let it be clearly understood that this
next plane is not "Heaven," or the conscious Presence
of God. Those people who work through great difficulties in this world and go over with an enlightened
consciousness, find themselves so much better off that
they sometimes think it must be Heaven; but it is not.
It is a limited etheric world—less limited than is this
plane, but limited nevertheless, and just as liable to
discord and decay. Indeed, objects over there decay
much more quickly than do objects on this plane. Instead of broken or worn-out objects lying about for a
long time as they do with us, the forms in which people
are no longer interested melt right back into the ether
immediately, and this makes new-comers think that
there is no decay there; but there is, only it is ended
much more quickly. In our world, for example, a chair,
let us say, or a suit of clothes, is manufactured, whereupon it immediately begins to wear out. This process,

however, is a very slow one, so much so that even after it becomes too shabby or damaged for further use, the fragments of it still lie about for years and years before falling into dust, if not otherwise disposed of. On the next plane a discarded etheric form fades out very quickly.

You do not "meet God" on the next plane any more than you do on this plane. God is everywhere. Of course, He is fully present on the next plane just as He is on this plane; but there as here, He is to be contacted only in one's own consciousness by some form of prayer or spiritual treatment. Heaven is that perfect state of consciousness in which one is in full realization of the Divine Presence. In that consciousness there is no limitation, or evil, or decay of any kind. When one attains to that condition he has finished with etheric planes just as surely as he has finished with the plane of physical matter. If you can reach to that level of consciousness while still in this world (and a few have succeeded in doing so), you do not "die" or go across to the etheric planes at all; you go straight to Heaven from this earth. Moses did this, and Enoch, and Elijah, and a few others. This is what is called translation or dematerialization. It is accomplished by the overcoming of the sense of separation from God which is really the "fall of man." It means overcoming selfishness, sensuality, criticism, fear, and other such things. It means living nearer and nearer to God every day. Of Enoch,* the Bible says, "he walked with God," before he was translated—and indeed there is no other way to freedom.

There are some very unpleasant localities in the next world (it is no use ignoring this fact just for senti-

*Genesis 5:24.

mental reasons), but the average person does not go to any of them. People who lead very evil lives on this earth, whose minds are chiefly given up to hatred, deceit, or sensuality, will find themselves in such places. This does not mean the average man or woman who may fall into wrong-doing under the pressure of severe temptation, but people whose whole lives are deliberately wrong. These are the places referred to as "hell" by the orthodox preachers. They are not places of vindictive punishment, and they certainly do not last forever, but only until the delinquent has seen the error of his ways and has reformed. Let me repeat that no one "sends" anyone to these places; they are merely the natural surroundings of a soul which has gotten itself into that condition by repeatedly choosing the lower in preference to the higher. Neither does anyone determine when the punishment will cease; the escape from such conditions takes place automatically as soon as the soul is sufficiently changed.

Someone may be inclined to ask whether it is appropriate to speak of "localities" on the next plane since such places are really but the out-picturing of the subject's own thoughts. The answer is that this is all that localities are on this plane. What we call a country, or a city, or a house, or a room, in this world is but out-pictured thought—nothing more—and indeed the only fundamental differences over there are the absence of inertia, which makes things happen almost instantaneously; and the existence of the extra dimension.

So it happens that once people wake up in the next world and begin to get used to the conditions, they usually have a great sense of physical well-being, and a most interesting and instructive life. The conditions of

living are utterly different from ours. There your
money is no longer of the slightest use to you—"you
can't take it with you"—and only the mental and spiritual wealth that you have accumulated can go along.
There is no money as we understand it because,
thought being immediately demonstrated, there is no
need to purchase objective possessions. What you are
able to think of clearly, you have. Many fine things will
still be out of the reach of many people there, because
they cannot clearly conceive them; and is not this the
exact truth about our own world also? In this world,
anything that you can clearly conceive comes into your
possession if you really want it, and anything that you
truly understand becomes yours in a still deeper sense,
for you never can lose it. The chief difference between
the two worlds is, once more, that results come so
much more slowly in this world, owing to the inertia of
physical matter, which over there they do not have to
meet.

There is no childbirth on the next plane, and therefore no marriage or family life as we understand it;
and when you consider the extraordinary importance
of the family on this plane, you will see that without it
the whole scheme of living must be different.

Will you meet your relatives and friends when you
go over? People naturally wonder whether they will
see again those whom they loved who have passed out
of sight; and to tell the truth, many are quite appre-
hensive of having to renew their contact with people
whom they have disliked—members of the family perhaps whom they would much prefer never to meet
again. The fact is, that where there is a strong emotional link either of love or hatred there is likely to be a
meeting. Where there is a strong link of genuine love

there is sure to be a meeting. Where there is no particular feeling between two people there will not be a meeting. Of course, love will take care of itself, but there is a real danger that if you allow yourself to indulge in hatred of anyone, you will meet when you have both passed over. To present this happening, destroy the link by ceasing to hate. Forgive the other person and set him free in your thought. You so not have go like him, but you must wish him well.*

Do not imagine that your family will ever be reassembled on the other side. Family relationships are for this plane only and have no existence there. Your father will not be your father on the other side, but a friend who played the role of father over here. Your daughter will not be your daughter there, but a friend who enacted the part of daughter to you for a number of years on the earth. Some people imagine that the whole earth family must be reassembled as a family over there; but consider what this would mean: You had two parents, and probably some brothers and sisters; each of your parents had two parents and probably some brothers and sisters; and so forth; and so you will see what the compulsory reunion of families would involve in a few generations. The actual fact is, as I have stated, that the relationships of parents and children, brothers and sisters, uncles and nephews, husbands and wives, are but temporary arrangements for this life only. If two brothers, or a parent and child, have a strong bond of sympathy in this life, they will meet again and perhaps be closely associated on the next plane; but this will be because of the bond of sympathy and not because they happened to be members of the same family here. When a marriage is satisfying

*See essay, *The Lord's Prayer*.

to both parties here, the partnership can continue by mutual consent on the other side; otherwise death dissolves a marriage, and the two need never even meet again, much less resume any kind of mutual bond.

Beyond the next plane there are other planes, and after a certain length of time over there most people develop mentally and spiritually so that they graduate out of that plane onto the next higher one. That plane has five dimensions, and the ether composing it is far less dense than that of the one next to us, and it in turn presents many new opportunities to the developing soul. After "death" one's instinct is to lead somewhat the same type of life as he has been accustomed to here, and this is why some intellectual or artistic training, and particularly some spiritual development, makes so much difference.

There is no limit over there to the opportunities for intellectual study and attainment. Most of the age-old, and to us insoluble, problems of philosophy and religion can be answered on the next plane with some study and trouble. Of course, this only means that new ones then come up for consideration, because, as we lengthen our vision so does the horizon but grow. Nevertheless, wonderful progress in the understanding of life can be, and is made along these lines. The artist and the musician at last begin to get things their own way. The lack of commercial aptitude which usually marks the genuine artist and for which he is so often punished in this world, is no detriment over there. And the etheric conditions present little or no difficulty such as physical matter does to the development of literary, artistic, and musical gifts. It is worth mentioning that even a little study along intellectual lines while in this world, and even a very little genuine interest in art or music is sufficient to start off the newcomer over there under very favorable auspices. On the other hand, those who know nothing whatever about these things find it much more difficult to make the beginning over there than they would here. Scientific studies such as chemistry, physics, electricity, and so forth, can be tremendously developed over there since the nature of vibration is far better understood on the other side than it is with us.

The man who benefits least by the change to the new world is the materially minded person who has developed no mental or spiritual resources whatever while on this plane. Being interested only in material things, in food and drink, and money, in social success, worldly honors, and material possessions in general, he naturally finds himself rather stranded in a world where none of these things have any meaning. Nevertheless, if he has led an average honest, clean life, and on the whole behaved decently according to his lights, he will be nothing worse than extremely bored until his higher faculties begin to unfold in the course of time.

Now consider the man or woman who lives wholly for the body and is dominated by it—the sensualist, the dipsomaniac, the drug addict. Physical cravings, being part of the mentality, are, of course, carried over to the next plane, but there there is no physical body through which these appetites may be satisfied, and so the victim is tormented by desire but unable to satisfy it, until, in the course of time, these desires fade out by starvation. This is the natural punishment for allowing the physical body to assume control, and surely it is punishment enough. Indeed, we find what is called poetic justice running right through the universe. The rewards of positive thought and action are the natural consequences following upon these things, and the punishments following upon wrong doing or neglect are natural consequences too. Like begets like. Take care of your body and you are rewarded with the joy of health, not with money. Take care of your business and you are rewarded with prosperity, not necessarily with health. Work hard at your music, and the reward is to be an accomplished musician; neglect it, and no money will buy the proficiency that you have failed to earn. Ill-treat your body, and the natural punishment is sickness and discomfort, not a falling-off in the value of your stocks and bonds. And so on through the whole gamut of life, we reap as we sow, whether it be on the earth plane or on any of the etheric planes which lie beyond. It may be said here that it is not necessary to lead an ascetic life in this world in order to be happy in the next one. All the ordinary harmless pleasures of life may be enjoyed in reasonable moderation without involving any suffering or hardship afterward.

It sometimes happens when a person "dies," that instead of his going into a coma immediately after the Silver Cord is broken, there may be an interval of hours or longer in which he retains full possession of his faculties; and sometimes he does not even realize that he is "dead," though as a rule he sees his physical body lying prone, and knows what has happened. In such cases he will make a strong effort to communicate with his closest friends. Suppose, for example, that a man died in the street, and retained his faculties in this way. He would immediately try to get home to his wife to tell her what had happened. Let us suppose that his home was ten miles away in the suburbs. Having now only an etheric body, he would really need but to think strongly of his home, and he would find himself there in a few seconds or less, because his etheric body could pass through houses, hills or any other physical obstruction that might lie in the way. As a matter of fact, however, habit might lead him to go through the motions of walking to the nearest railroad station and getting into a train, or he might clamber onto a street car. On entering his home he would instinctively shout to his wife, but having no physical organs, no sound would be produced—the effort would be purely mental and she would hear nothing. He would then probably walk over to her and attempt to grasp her arm. But his etheric substance would simply pass through it without making any impression. It might happen, however, in such a case that the strong mental effort would reach the consciousness of the wife or whomever he was endeavoring to reach, and then she would afterward say: "My husband appeared to me for a moment at the time he was killed." His thought would be so charged with emotion that it would be strong enough, upon reaching her, to cause her to project a momentary thought form of him. It might, however, not be strong enough for this, and then she would merely say: "I knew that something had happened to my husband long before I got the news." This is the explanation of most such stories which are so constantly met with.

In the same way, people have sometimes attended their own funerals before passing over. It is worthy of note that, since death makes no general change in us, those who possess a sense of humor retain it, and those who do not, continue in the lack; and on such an occasion as this, those who do possess that useful gift are sometimes much amused at the proceedings, and those without it react also as might be expected.

Where there is a strong sense of bereavement; or where the survivors are left in tragic circumstances, the dead person will of course suffer acutely. As a matter of fact, the so-called dead are very sensitive to our thoughts for a considerable time after they have passed over to the other side, and for this reason *excessive grief is to be deprecated.* It saddens them and prevents their focusing their attention as they should upon the new life which they are starting. Of course, it seems very hard to tell people not to grieve when one whom they have dearly loved passes out of sight; but the fact remains that excessive grief is bad for both parties. Remember that if there is a link of love you will certainly meet again, and that nothing that is good, or beautiful, or true, can ever be lost. On this plane we often see our friends or our dearly loved ones go away to live in a distant country knowing that we shall not see them again for several years—and death is really nothing more than this. Here I would impress upon those who are responsible for the support of others—husbands or fathers of families, for instance—the duty of making what reasonable provision they can for those who may be left behind without resources in case of their unexpected decease. It will save them a great deal of remorse and self-reproach on the other side if they can feel that at least they did what lay in their power to ease the burden of those who were dependent upon them.

At this point it may be well to explain that when a person is passing on, the body often undergoes violent twitchings and contortions, and most distressing moans may be emitted. This, however, need cause no uneasiness because such actions are purely reflex—the patient is totally unaware of them and is slipping gently and comfortably away.

In a very small proportion of cases it happens that after death people become what is called "earth-bound," which means that they remain on this plane for an indefinite length of time, being unable to go on. This is simply due to the fact that their emotions are so fixed on something in this world, that they cannot fall into the coma in which one passes across. It is exactly parallel to the case of a person who cannot fall asleep at night because his mind is so full of some dominating interest. A man can be so emotionally bound up with something here that he cannot get his attention off it even when he loses his body. Such an absorbing interest may be a piece of property, or it may be a person, or it may be some dominating activity, or it may be a crime which he committed here. In the last case his thoughts anchor him to the neighborhood of the scene of the crime. As time goes on, this effect fades out and he passes over, sooner or later, but in extreme cases it may last for quite a long time. The moral of this, of course, is that you must not allow any one thing in the world to monopolize your attention to the exclusion of all other interests.

The one thing that is worthy of unlimited devotion is the search for God; but this can possess our lives and yet never make us unbalanced. Nor does this mean that we ought to go through life without taking very much interest in anything in particular, for such a life simply would not be worth living. On the contrary, we should take a strong interest in all the events of life as they come to us, and the more things we are interested in the better it will be, provided that interest is within the bounds of reason. In particular, we should be en-thusiastically interested in our daily work, whatever it may be; but again—always within the bounds of reason. Nothing must have such a strangling grip upon the heart that the loss of that particular thing would make the rest of our lives to be meaningless. This is the true understanding of the Eastern virtue of *detachment*, namely, a keen, intelligent interest in the things which are with us while they are with us, with complete readiness to pass on to new things when the signal comes. Living in this way there will never be any possibility of being earth-bound.

We can pray for those who have passed on, and indeed it is a sacred duty to do so. Prayers for the so-called dead have been used in most parts of the world in most ages. The practice was generally discontinued after the Reformation because it had been greatly abused and commercialized, but, nevertheless, it is an excellent practice in itself. You should pray for your friend who has passed on exactly as you would pray for him if he were living in some distant spot on this globe, say China or South Africa. Realize peace of mind, freedom, and understanding for him, and that God is Life, and Intelligence, and Love. *The Presence* is excellent for his purpose. Read it to him silently, saying, "You" where the text says "I."

Now I come to the problem of the disposal of dead bodies and of funeral arrangements in general. Here let me say bluntly that most of our accepted burial customs are really pagan survivals and are wanting both in intelligence and in decency. We tolerate them only because we are more or less accustomed to them, and, indeed, when it comes about that thoughtful people attend a conventional funeral for the first time, they are invariably both shocked and repelled. The whole thing really implies that the deceased person is there in the grave, although hardly anybody nowadays believes that. Why Christians, who profess to believe in the immortality of the soul, should treat the physical remains as though they were something sacred, passes comprehension. Such an attitude is neither logical nor intelligent.

You should realize this fact very clearly—there is nothing whatever sacred about a dead body. It is a collection of physical matter for which the ex-owner has no further use, and it should be disposed of in as cleanly and expeditious a manner as possible, and that is all. Its late owner wore out a number of physical bodies during his life (as you probably know, we get a number of new bodies by gradual replacement as we go through life), and this is only the last of them that is being buried ceremoniously, that is all. Remember that the beauty of a beautiful body comes from the soul that shines through it, and does not lie in the body itself. That soul with its beauty and joy has now gone on, and the body left is but an old garment which has been discarded. This garment should be disposed of (for the sake of the living) with respect, but not with reverence; and the proper method of doing this is by cremation. One should be quite clear about this. The disposal of the body is simply a duty to the living and not in any way an honor to the deceased who takes no further interest in it. Fire is cleanly, purifying, and respectful. The body should be cremated after a lapse of about three days, except in cases where rapid decomposition has set in, when cremation may take place immediately.

The body having been cremated, it is better not to preserve the ashes. Only a morbid satisfaction can come from keeping these gruesome relics. They should be scattered over some growing grass, or

thrown on the sea, or on a river or lake; of course, with
a prayer. For the same reason monuments of any kind
in cemeteries are out of place and should if it is at all
possible, be avoided, even where family considerations
have made burial unavoidable. A little reflection will
show you that to erect a monument over a cast-off
body is just as unreasonable as it would be for you to
bury an old suit of clothes and then put a monument
over that.

Certainly you should avoid visiting the grave of your
loved one. You know that he is not in the cemetery; so
keep away from it. Pray for him in the sanctuary of
your own home. No other place is any more sacred or
more appropriate for prayer than your home. On his
birthday, or any to her significant anniversary, have a
bunch of flowers in remembrance of him, but let this
be done at home and not in the graveyard. If you happen to have a portrait of him, you can put the flowers
in front of that. Of course, this should only be done
occasionally and not kept up as an everyday practice.

You should avoid wearing mourning. Do not swathe
yourself in black for the sake of your loved one who is
not dead but very much alive; and at this point I may
mention that it is not well, in a general way, to keep
personal things belonging to the deceased, if you are
doing this in a sentimental or morbid spirit. Here you
will need discrimination. There is no objection to
keeping a few mementoes if you are certain that you
are not doing it in the spirit of mourning, thinking that
he is dead. On the other hand, the idea of maintaining
his room or his books, and so forth, "just as he left
them," as some people do, is completely wrong and pagan. The deceased would not wish it, and would probably laugh good-naturedly at you if he could make you

know it. All conditions belonging to the past should, as far as possible, be broken up to make way for the living present.

Here I wish to explain that while the foregoing instructions are what really should be done, yet in certain cases it will not be possible, for family reasons, to carry them out. If other members of your family are old-fashioned in their views, particularly the older members—parents, for instance—then it is often well to give way and do what they expect, rather than wound their deepest feelings. It may be that while you know better, they do not; and so if cremation would shock them, have the body buried and attend the funeral in the name of Christian charity. Of course, the expressed wish of the deceased should always be carried out. We should do all that we can within reason to avoid giving pain in these matters to parents and older relatives. On the other hand, do not compromise in order to spare the feelings of young people, because they ought to learn better; and never consider the opinions of neighbors or distant relatives in such matters.

A man in New York told me that he was not wearing black because he knew that his recently deceased sister was not dead, but that on visiting his parents' home which he did every few weeks, he wore mourning to avoid scandalizing them. I told him that he was quite right, and that such was the course I always advised in these matters.

A word had better be said here about suicide. The majority of those who take their own lives are so worried or terrorized at the time that they are not morally responsible for the act, and so it is not really suicide but rather death by misadventure. Such people fare on

the other side like anyone else. In a genuine case of suicide, however, it is very different. Conscious and intentional self-destruction is a crime severely punished
by Nature. It is a refusal to meet the problems of life,
and obviously it cannot be possible to do that successfully. Those who seek this way out do not meet their
friends on the other side. They are lonely and unhappy and are apt to find themselves in a confused
mental state which is really subjective—a kind of
vague dream which sometimes makes them think they
are wandering about in a dense fog. Of course, they
can be greatly helped by prayer as can all others. Ultimately they have to face all over again precisely the
kind of problem they have run away from, with time
wasted and suffering experienced for nothing.

Now I reach the problem of whether it is possible or
not to communicate with those who have passed on
into the next world. On this subject an enormous number of books have been published, and a most acrimo-
nious and bitter controversy has raged up and down
the world for a very long time. Indeed, many people
seem unable to touch on this subject and at the same
time retain either their common sense or their good
manners. The most violent epithets are hurled at one
another by controversialists on both sides, and I have
known several long standing friendships to be severed
over just this question of whether or not it is possible
for us to communicate with the so-called dead. Ex-
tremists on one side say dogmatically that it is absolutely impossible to do so. Enthusiasts on the other side
claim that they are in clear and intimate communication with their deceased friends as frequently as once
or twice a week or more. What is the truth? Well, the
truth is that communication does occasionally take

place, but that it is far rarer than most believers in it suppose, and that it is always accomplished with considerable difficulty and uncertainty. It is not in the least like telephoning from New York to Chicago. It is more like the very early days of Marconi's experiments in wireless when an occasional and very broken message came through; but much more often mere atmospheric disturbances and meaningless movements of the instruments were all that could be registered.

Do not dabble in psychic things. If you wish to investigate thoroughly and scientifically, well and good, but this will be the work of years, and will call for scientific conditions. The chief objection to the running after mediums that so many people practise is that it is really a running away from the responsibilities of this life. Professional mediums say that they seldom get a client who is happy, whose life is full of prosperity and self-expression. On the contrary, it is those whose lives here are frustrated and unhappy, irrespective of a particular bereavement, who are always trying to communicate with the next plane. Thus it becomes what is called in psychology, an escape mechanism, and it can be almost as disastrous as taking to drink or narcotic drugs. Your business is to live here in this world while you are here; to face up to your problems here and to try to solve them; and to live in the next world when you get there.

There is a truly spiritual mode of communication from which nothing but good can come. It is this: Sit down quietly and remind yourself that the one God really is Omnipresent. Then reflect that your Real Self—the Divine Spark of you—is in the Presence of God now, and that the Real Self—the Divine Spark—of your loved one is also in the Presence of God. Do his for a few minutes every day, and sooner or later you will get a sense of communication. However, no detailed message will come, as a rule—only a definite and unmistakable sense that he knows you have thought of him and that he is thinking of you.

People often ask what they should do to prepare themselves for the next world. The best way to prepare for the future is to live rightly today. Lead a clean, honest life, embodying in your conduct the highest that you know at the time. Be as useful as you can to others. Do all that you can to help other people in any way that is open to you. Everyone has some opportunity of service—physical, mental, or spiritual—and these opportunities must be used. If you seem to have no opportunities to help others, go to work and manufacture some.

Learn the Truth of Being. Learn as much as you can about the nature of God—the only thing really worth knowing—and learn what man is, and what life really means.

This world is a school, that and nothing more, and provided you learn your lesson, nothing else matters. It does not really matter whether you are rich or poor, cultured or simple, a king or a scavenger. These are only the roles that men enact on the stage of life. How the role is acted is what matters. The two supreme lessons set for this school are the lesson of the Omnipresence of God, and the lesson of the power of thought. Every negative or difficult thing that enters into your life marks your inability to realize the Presence of God at that point, and it is therefore but the signal for another step to be made. Make that step in spiritual understanding, and never again throughout eternity will that particular task have to be done.

The power of thought is the second great lesson that we have to master, and here again, as Jesus told us, the tree is known by its fruits.

Now that you understand these things in some degree, it should be possible for you to go through life and to meet death with that "even mind" to which a modern seer referred. You should be habitually cheerful and happy, neither unduly elated by seeming good fortune, nor unduly depressed by temporary adversity—because you assess both of these things at their correct value. You should never be so completely wedded to any particular set of conditions—to a house, or a district, or a job, or a vocation, or to any earthly arrangement—that you cannot part from it without undue regret. You should not be dependent for your happiness or self-respect upon human praise or approval, though such things may be appreciated in their place. Your attitude should be:

I do my duty and enjoy myself where I am; I do my job and pass on—to another. I am going to live forever; in a thousand years from now I shall still be alive and active somewhere; in a hundred thousand years still alive and still active somewhere else; and so the events of today have only the importance that belongs to today. Always the best is yet to be. Always the future will be better than the present or the past because I am ever growing and progressing, and I am an immortal soul. I am the master of my fate. I greet the unknown with a cheer, and press forward joyously, exulting in the Great Adventure.

Armed with this philosophy, and really understanding its power, you have nothing to fear in life or death—because God is All, and God is Good.

NOTE

I would impress upon readers of this essay that no written description can really do justice to the subject. It can but hint and suggest the truth.

However *correct* the itinerary of a journey may be, it is likely to seem somewhat dry and unattractive when read, since the beauty and joy of the new adventure must evade the written word.

This essay, of course, describes the experiences of the soul between incarnations.

REINCARNATION

THE IMPRISONED SPLENDOUR

Truth is within ourselves; it takes no rise from
outward things, what e'er you may believe.
There is an inmost center in us all,
Where truth abides in fulness; and around,
Wall upon wall, the gross flesh hems it in,
This perfect clear perception—which is truth.
A baffling and perverting carnal mesh
Binds it, and makes all error; and to know
Rather consists in opening out a way
Whence the imprisoned splendour may escape,
Than in effecting entry for a light
Supposed to be without.

Browning

Reincarnation

HAVE you ever asked yourself why there should be such a difference between one human lot and another? Have you ever wondered why some people seem to be so happy and fortunate in their lives, while others appear to undergo so much undeserved suffering? I am sure you have, because only a very selfish or a very thoughtless person could fail to be challenged sooner or later by this problem.

Why is one person so well placed in life, having apparently everything done for him; being born into a nice family, carefully brought up, given every advantage that money and culture can confer, sent to good schools, and launched into life with every advantage?

Why is another boy or girl born into very difficult circumstances, where it is all but impossible to make any advance in life?

Why is one child born a cripple, or born blind, or born with some horrible disease, while another child arrives in this world with a strong, clean, healthy little body, certain to grow up well and sturdy?

Why does one child reach manhood or womanhood, and live to a ripe old age, whereas another child is born, and after only a few weeks, or a few months, or even a few years, dies, without seemingly having lived to any purpose? In a certain old country churchyard, there is a tombstone dating from the seventeenth century. It marks the grave of an infant who died after three weeks, and the epitaph reads: *Since so soon done, why was I begun?* And, indeed, the question is an extremely searching one.

Such questions call urgently for an answer if we are to believe in the existence of God, and in a universe governed by law and order. To the honest and fearless soul, the problem of the inequality of human lives is one that clamors for solution.

Men and women are not born free and equal. They are *created* free and equal, but they are not *born* so. The Declaration of Independence does not say that men are *born* free and equal. It says that they are *created* so, which is quite a different thing. Men and women are not born free and equal but start this life like horses in a handicap race—no two bearing an equal burden. Now, why should this be, if indeed God is Love, and if God is just, and if God is all powerful?

Well, the answer is that this life that you are living today is not the only life; and that it cannot be understood when judged by itself. The answer is that you have lived before, not once, but many, many times, and that in the course of these many lives you have *thought* and *said* and *done* all sorts of things, good and bad, and that the circumstances into which you were born are but the natural outcome of the way in which you have lived and comported yourself in your former lives. You are reaping today, for good or evil, the results of the seeds that you have sown during these many previous lives. The Bible says, "Whatsoever a man soweth, that shall he also reap"; and that text states the truth, and it cannot be made to mean anything else.

You who read these words have lived many, many times before, in different ages, in different conditions, under different skies, and in different civilizations. Many times you have been a man, and many times you have been a woman. You have probably been very rich, and very poor; and probably, you have sometimes been highly placed in the world, and sometimes your place has been lowly. Some of those who are at the bottom of our social ladder today have walked the earth as kings, and presidents, and generals, and admirals, and high priests; and some who now sit in the seats of the mighty, surrounded by pomp and circumstance, have toiled as simple peasants in days gone by, pulled at the oar of a galley, or worn the chains of the slave. And you, yourself, in future ages, centuries from now very likely, will return to this earth planet and be born again as a baby in some family; and grow up, and probably marry, and live out another life. And the conditions under which you start that life will be the outcome of the lives you have already lived; but most particularly will they be the outcome of the life which you are living at the present time. That, briefly, is the story of the life of man. What is customarily called a lifetime is really but a comparatively brief day in a long, long life.

This is the glorious truth, and it is the most wonderful and beautiful thing that you could ever discover. It is the door of liberation. It is your Charter of Freedom, your passport to Fullness of Life. It means nothing less than that your destiny is in your own hands, and that you may determine that destiny—that you may really make your future life, beginning today, the sort of thing that you wish it to be.

You arrived in this world as a tiny baby, unconscious; and then came consciousness with the first breath; and then your new life and had begun. Probably the first thing that happened to you when you came into the world was that they spanked you, and in most cases, until you know the Law and practise it, the world will go on spanking you until the very end—until nature gets tired of you and turns you out. You came into the world with a cry—with the very first breath you drew you gave a cry—and many people spend their whole lives crying and protesting, right down to the grave. When, however, you understand that this present life is only one day in your *long life*, and that at the change called death you simply disappear onto the next plane, to come back again later on, then the events of this particular life appear in their true proportion, *and then you begin to have dominion.* The events of this life will not appear less important because of your new knowledge, but they will no longer intimidate you, because you will know that you can control them. No seeming misfortune will any longer have power to break your heart or weaken your courage. You will understand life as the wondrous opportunity and the glorious gift that it is.

People often say that they are sick of this life anyway, that they do not like the world, and that they do not want to come back; but this attitude usually arises from a misunderstanding. It is not really this earth life that they dislike, but the limited or unsatisfactory conditions in which they are finding themselves at present. They fail to realize that they will not, in any case, come back to anything like their present conditions.

You, personally, will probably come back again; but you are not likely to come back for five hundred years or so anyway, and so, obviously, you will not come back to the world you know today. You will return to a very different world, with different conditions, different ways of life, different institutions, different food, and clothing, and social customs, and, above all, to a world full of new and different problems. Most, if not all, of mankind's present problems will have been worked out in one way or another by that time. Most, if not all, existing institutions will have disappeared. All the things that you dislike or disapprove of in the world today will have gone, but, by the same token, most or all of the things that you particularly like and approve of will have gone too—and so when you do arrive it will be for a completely fresh start. It is true that you will have to meet the same *types* of problems, the fundamental types that arise out of the essential character of human nature; but the *conditions* will be utterly different; and the experiences of this life, and all the things that you learned this time will be with you, and will stand you in good stead.

You will not only come back, but you will probably meet some of your present associates again, particularly if there is an emotional link either of love or hatred between you. Love will take care of itself; but you must get all hatred out of your heart, if you do not want to renew disagreeable contacts.*

In the same way, some of your present associates are sure to be people with whom you had dealings in a previous life or lives. Your son today may have been your father, or merely an acquaintance in days gone by, and a close friend today may in other times have been a relative or a husband, or wife. The general tendency is for people who live and move in the same groups to reincarnate about the same time, though, of course, there will always be exceptions.

*See essay, *The Lord's Prayer*.

I said that you personally will *probably* come back again, and here the question naturally arises—*is it absolutely necessary to come back?* Must we positively come back whether we wish to or not, or however strongly we may prefer not to? And the answer is, no, it is not absolutely necessary to come back, but the only way to avoid doing so is a way that hardly anyone will take. You need not come back if you will concentrate your whole heart upon God, seek His presence until you realize it *vividly,* and live to do His Holy Will, and that alone; first, last, and all the time. If you can really do this, and it is of all tasks the most difficult, then you will leave this earth planet to enter into full communion with God, and you need never come back. You will be, as the Bible says, a pillar in the house of God, and need go out no more. Hardly anyone, however, is really prepared to do this at present, and so we have to go on by stages, gradually getting nearer to God as the ages go by, learning slowly from experience or rapidly through study, prayer, and meditation; living life after life until at last we "grow up" spiritually—when the day breaks and the shadows flee away.

The reason why the Bible nowhere definitely teaches Reincarnation and, in fact, avoids the subject, is because the Bible teaches us to concentrate on the task of achieving our reunion with God instead of postponing this indefinitely as many Eastern people do. The doctrine of Reincarnation when not thoroughly understood sometimes tends to make people apathetic and fatalistic. The Bible encourages men to seek actively to liberate themselves from all limitations.

At the same time, it must be remembered that this earth life can be a most interesting and joyous process in itself, for this is a wonderful world (of which even

now man only knows about five per cent) and your so-
journ here can be a series of wonderful and joyous ad-
ventures, if only you will learn the laws of life and
apply them. You are not obliged to be sick, or sad, or
lonely, or frustrated, or unsuccessful. This life and the
lives that follow it can be made interesting, and joyous,
and free.

When I speak of seeking whole-heartedly for God,
and putting Him first, I do not mean that you have to
spend all your time in church-going, or even in prayer
and meditation. That would be unwise. It would be
doing as the Anchorites and Hermits of ancient times
did. They went into the desert, or climbed on top of a
tall pillar to be alone, to get away from temptation
and difficulty—but that is not the way. In most cases
they merely spent the time in thinking about themselves all day long, and this naturally brought serious
troubles upon them. Progress is made by overcoming
the practical difficulties of our everyday lives, not by
running away from them. Jesus, knowing this, said
that he would not pray that his followers should be
taken out of the world, but rather than they should
remain in the world and develop naturally there.
And, indeed, that is just what the world is for. Practical life is the school for spiritual development and the
overcoming of selfishness and fear. Your duty is to fill
your place in life, whatever it may be for the time being, to the very best of your ability, and to try sincerely to live up to the highest that you know at the
moment.

Of course, a definite time must be set aside daily for
prayer and meditation, but the rest of the time must be
used for incorporating your spiritual understanding
into your practical life; for thus only can you yourself

progress and help the world too.* So, far from being a recluse or an Anchorite, you can make friends, go about the world, visit the theatre, read the newspapers, travel abroad, join clubs and associations, and do all the customary things that people do, but you must do them in the light of your spiritual understanding. Your understanding must mould your activities and your environment; you must not allow your environment to mould you. You must live, so far as you can, as consciously the expression of God, and as His witness and representative.

Why is Reincarnation necessary? Why should life have to develop in that particular way? The reason is this: We are here on the earth planet to learn certain lessons. We are here to develop spiritually. We are here to acquire full understanding of and control over our mentality; and this cannot be done in one lifetime. Why not? Why do we come back, and back, and back many times to this earth for short excursions of perhaps seventy or eighty years instead of, let us say, finishing it up in one very long lifetime of perhaps a thousand or even several thousand years? The explanation lies in man's mental laziness and inertia; in his reluctance to change himself radically, to pull himself out of a rut when once he gets into it, to adopt new ideas and adapt himself to changing conditions. The explanation lies in man's conservatism and tendency to self-satisfaction and, above all, in his ignorance of his own unlimited potentialities—and these are just the very things that he is here to overcome.

Consider again the life of man as we know it in almost every case. He arrives as a newborn baby with no conscious memory of the past. Even his consciousness

*The Fifteen Points (page 272).

of the present is at first very limited. Then gradually that consciousness expands and he begins to know his surroundings, to recognize his mother or his nurse. He smiles at them and understands their smiles and caresses. He begins to learn elementary facts concerning life on this plane. He learns to judge distances by feeling out with his hands, discovering that he can touch the side of the cradle, but not the ceiling. He experiences both hunger and satisfaction, both pain and bodily ease.

Gradually he learns to talk, and with the equipment of even a few words his means of communication and of control over his little life is immensely enhanced. He learns the very difficult business of walking. (You have forgotten about it now, but it was a terrible job at the time, that learning to balance and to walk. You tumbled about and bumped your head and cut your knees for a while, but presently you got tired of that and learned to walk safely.) Presently the baby learns to read and to write. These again are very difficult accomplishments—at the time. (You scribble off a letter now, or you skim through a newspaper at great speed, but there was a time when words like "cat" and "dog" presented a real difficulty either to read or write.)

The child goes on learning. Being young, he is interested in everything and wants to know about everything. He pesters his elders with questions on every conceivable subject. (Parents are never tired of telling about their children's thirst for knowledge. "What do you think Johnny asked his father last night?" mother will say.) So the child has this insatiable curiosity, the ceaseless desire to see everything and go everywhere and handle and experiment with everything. We call it play, or getting into mischief, but it really means tasting and investigating life.

So he grows and expands, goes through school and perhaps college, and then out into the world. Here the same process continues. He seeks new experience, wants to do things in new ways, look at old things with a fresh mind, *and wants to improve everything.* Of course he gets snubbed and rebuffed a good deal, but at first he does not allow this to daunt him. He is young, in the twenties let us say, and to be young is just this very thing. To be young is to have this interest and joy in living for its own sake, to have this appetite for new ideas and new ways, this freedom from fixed mental habits and emotional commitments. That is youth, and that is the consciousness where the morning stars sing together and the children of God shout for joy.

But presently something happens. The glory that is youth lasts for a time, and then . . . and then . . . well then something else begins to happen. That avid interest in all things, that readiness for the new and the untried, begins—insensibly at first—to fade a little, and discouragements and disappointments of one kind or another gradually begin to tell.

The strong race suggestions all around him gradually get their way. He begins to acquire vested interests (mentally) in the status quo. He begins to settle down. He drops emotional anchors into the sea of life, and these things lead, psychologically, to a diminution of energy. The idea of letting-well-enough-alone begins to appeal to him—and the malignant disease called middle age has set in.

As a boy of twelve he thought he could do anything he wanted to do, reasonable or unreasonable, from being a lion tamer in the circus or the driver of a fire engine, to President of the country. At twenty he thought he could do anything within reason—and he probably could. He might be a little nervous about it, but in his heart of hearts he really thought that he could do anything that any other fellow could do— and that is youth. When he read or heard of some brilliant achievement, no matter how magnificent, he whispered to himself "Well, I could do that too"—and that is youth. But "shades of the prison house begin to close about the growing boy," and now the time has come when he thinks instead, "How wonderful that is; of course I could never do anything like that; I am not in that class; I haven't the ability, or the training, or the money, or the right contact," or else, "It is now too late." That is middle age, and it comforts itself with all kinds of promises and deceptions and foolish rationalizations as the wheels of life slow down toward the end.

Now you will see that nature could have no object in keeping this middle-aged man alive for hundreds or thousands of years, because he is no longer of much use to her. Nature wants to do new things in new ways, always something new and something better; and the crystallized mentality is not ready for this. So her only remedy, when crystallization sets in, is to remove him from the earth plane altogether; send him to the etheric planes for rest, reflection, assimilation, and general readjustment; and then bring him back again once more as a baby, to experience a new youth and a new period of true spiritual production.

There are other reasons why the reincarnating of the ego many times is necessary, although they really arise from the fact which we have just been considering. Nature wants you to have all kinds of experience in order to develop every side of your character. You need to have been a man and you need to have been a woman, to have been a parent and also a child. You need to learn lessons of discipline and self-restraint, and you need to learn to use authority in the right way. You need to learn the lesson of getting on with other people, and you must also learn to be alone. You must learn to value health and rational living even if you have to learn it through the discipline of sickness. You must learn to bear failure and disappointment with fortitude and you must learn to stand success without allowing your head to be turned. You have to develop such an understanding faith in the unseen that you can find the things that are seen slipping away from you without panic. You have to learn the lesson of patience, and the lesson of enterprise and adventure too; and, above all, you have to move about in time and space that you may learn that nothing that God made is really strange or foreign or separate—and this could not be done in one incarnation.

This is why Reincarnation is necessary. You will see now what a simple and natural process it is. The idea seems a strange and startling one at first only because we in the West have been totally unaware of it. But in the East it is as familiar a fact as the rising and setting of the sun, and it is probable that the majority of mankind have always believed in Reincarnation.

People who accept this truth sometimes prefer to call it by another name—Reproduction, Counterfesance, or Metempsychosis, or some other title—but the principle is the same; the reappearance on the earth of the same individual, time after time.

Why do you not remember your previous lives? Well, you do not remember the early days of this life. For various reasons Nature has drawn a veil of forgetfulness over our beginnings on this plane, and for excellent reasons she hides away the memory of previous lives until we are sufficiently developed to be ready to remember them. It would not be well for most people to be able to recollect their previous lives, because at the present time they simply could not stand it. Consider how prone people are to worry and grieve foolishly over the past events of this one life. Think how they fume and fret over some incident of twenty years ago when they themselves said or did something rather foolish, or when someone else ill-treated them, or what-not. Think how they sentimentalize and mope over "the dear dead days of long ago"; and imagine the state they would get themselves into if they had the material of many lives to handle in this way. Obviously they would destroy themselves very quickly.

The woman who cannot forget or at least forgive a mistake her husband made twenty years ago, would have a bad time with the memories of all the mistakes made by even a dozen husbands or wives in the past. The man who cannot overlook the bitter thing that his wife said ten years ago, or forgive some grievance which he holds against one of his parents, could hardly survive the accumulated remembrance of many husbands, many wives, and many parents.

And so the past is mercifully withheld from us until we reach the stage when we can regard our own histories impersonally and objectively, and when we do reach that stage it is possible to remember our previous lives. This very faculty of being able to look at our own lives in a detached way, to consider impersonally our own deeds and the things done to us by others is one of the most difficult of all things to acquire. Indeed, most people who have not studied philosophy would not even dream that such a thing could be, and yet some day you will have to attain to this, and some day you will. A time will come when you will be able to look back and consider every incident in all your lives with great interest but as calmly and unconcernedly as though they had happened to the man next door. That is the prelude to Liberation. Meanwhile, some people do get an occasional glimpse of their past incarnations in one way or another, and, if wisely handled, such glimpses can be extremely useful. And there are those who get more than a glimpse.

As a matter of fact, the whole history of all your past lives is stored away in the deeper levels of your subconscious, and thus it is that your mentality today—and consequently your destiny—is the logical outcome of all the lives that you have lived up to the present.

> Our deeds still travel with us from afar,
> And what we have been, makes us what we are.

Now we must consider the question of how the baby comes to be born in the particular family in which it is born; how you, for example, came to be born into the particular family into which you were born. Let us consider how you came to be a Jones, or a Dumont, or a Hapsburg, or whatever you are. Why, out of all the races and nations and families on the globe, were you born in just that particular family where you were born? Let me begin by saying that the stork never makes a mistake. Each one of us is born into the conditions which exactly fit his soul at the time of incarnation. He naturally gravitates to the exact spot that belongs to him.

Of course, we do not choose our parents. We go to the parent whose nature and conditions correspond with the state of the soul when it incarnates. And often that family is anything but what we would choose at that time.

It should be understood that incarnation takes place at the moment of conception. When the male principle punctures the ovum, it sets up a powerful vortex in the finer ethers, and a soul is, so to speak, sucked onto this plane and attached to the fertilized cell. Just before this the soul was waiting on the next (etheric) plane ready to incarnate. It was at that time fully conscious and it had a clear recollection of its recent life on the etheric planes, and of the main events of its last earth life. Now it is drawn onto this plane and attached to the fertilized ovum which is the nucleus of its new body. For a moment it has a preview of what the general conditions of its new life will be, and then it falls into a state of coma from which it only begins to emerge when it is born, and from which it does not completely emerge until the age of puberty.

The subconscious mind is active all the time and from the moment of incarnation it is busily building the new body, for it is the baby's own subconscious that builds its body in the uterus, and it builds it in its own image and likeness—that is why our bodies express the things that are in the soul. The mother supplies the material but the child's own soul builds its little body, and we learn in metaphysics that our environment is always but the out-picturing of our soul.

No one "sent" you to that family or selected it for you. Being the soul that you were, it was as natural and indeed as inevitable that you should go there, as it is natural for a certain drop of water on the Continental Divide to find its way ultimately into the Pacific or into the Atlantic, according to circumstances. Always remember that at the moment before birth, one is dealing, not with a new soul, but with a mature soul—the product of many lives. That soul has certain dominant characteristics, both good and bad, and under the Cosmic Law that *Like Attracts Like,* it finds its own place. Now its own place is not only the place that fits it at the time, but it is the very place that furnishes it with just the opportunity it needs to develop still further its good qualities and to overcome its weaknesses, if it so desires.

The soul gravitated to that particular family because at the beginning of its present life it had certain fundamental things in common with it. It is true that sometimes a child seems to be very much out of place in its family, but this is only an appearance. Underneath there is a fundamental family resemblance or the child would not be there. It is also true that as children grow up they usually grow apart from one another and from their parents, but, nevertheless, at the time of incarnation, there were certain fundamental similarities. Again, it is true that children are often drawn into their families by what it called a karmic link, as I shall describe later on. But this link is merely another aspect of the fact that like attracts life.

As with most of the laws of nature, the law of Reincarnation is simple in outline but extremely complicated in detail. Nevertheless, for practical purposes, a general understanding is quite sufficient. Your soul is extremely complicated. The whole of your environment and all your experiences are but the out-picturing of some of its aspects, for most of it has not come into manifestation yet. One aspect of your soul is clearly seen in your physical body, and certain underlying similarities with your parents and brothers and sisters come out in what we call family likenesses—family features and family mannerisms. Of course, we pick up many of these things by copying our elders while we are still young, but some are obviously inborn.

Now we are ready to understand the startling statement that *there is no such thing as heredity*. This statement will surprise many, but it is true. No one ever "inherits" anything from his parents or his ancestors. He already had certain mental tendencies before he incarnated this time and these tendencies guided him to a family where similar tendencies existed—that is all. The gouty subject, or the soul predisposed by its own nature to produce weak lungs, gravitates to the family having these conditions. One does not "inherit" gout or tuberculosis from his father or his grandmother; he joins a family of that type because he already has these conditions potentially. Like attracts like all through the universe, or, as we say more picturesquely, *birds of a feather flock together*.

John, with a mental quality that produces weak lungs, or gout, or a certain type of face, is taken by the stork to a family in which such mental qualities are common and which therefore out-pictures these things; but that is just his opportunity to overcome the tendency to gout or tuberculosis, or to overcome or develop the particular characteristic which produces that type of face. If he does this once and for all, he will never have to meet that problem again; but he has free will and if he is foolish he will probably do nothing about it, and postpone that overcoming to a future time. It often happens, of course, that a particular child arrives in a family noted for some so-called hereditary ailment, and yet is quite free from it, though his brothers and sisters do not escape. This only means that this particular soul was not subject to that physical weakness but had other characteristics in common with that family. Jane, whose trouble is emotional instability, lands in a rather hysterical family in the same way, and this too furnishes her with just the material for understanding and overcoming her own weakness, if she wants to.

Thomas has certain lessons to learn which call for the struggles and difficulties that the humble people of the world have to meet, whereas William, who has already overcome these, is born into easy and comfortable circumstances—though, note carefully, he now has to learn to handle these conditions, and this may be a more difficult lesson than that of Thomas. Also William, though he is now in affluent circumstances, may someday be re-born as poor as Thomas if he does not in this life make good use of the prosperity that is his.

Social standing and human learning are of no importance in themselves except as they provide opportunities for the growth in wisdom of the soul. They come and go throughout the *long life* in accordance with the need of the day. The simple laboring man of today may well have been a prince in days gone by, a prince maybe who led a good and useful life in his own sphere but needed certain lessons that are only to be learned among the rank and file—and, incidentally, he may well be a far happier man now. The reigning prince of today may yesterday have been a poor fisherman who qualified in that character for a larger rôle upon the stage of life. We must never seek to gauge eternal values by the passing standards of time. So you yourself are your own ancestors, and at some time or other you have produced your own personal character; and all your external conditions arise out of that.

So we see how absurd it really is for people to be, as they often are, either stupidly proud or stupidly ashamed of their parents or their home. We may well be rightly proud of spiritual growth, and especially of any rapid progress that we may make, but outer conditions are in themselves of no importance. We may be wisely proud of having had worthy parents, of course, because it proves that there must have been worth in us to have deserved to have parents like that. And it is for us to see to it that we do them credit.

Reincarnation explains at once the differences in talents which we find between one man and another, just as it explains all the other differences. Why has one man a special aptitude for music, another for engineering, and yet a third for farming, while so many seem to have no particular aptitude at all? Differences in talent, like differences in opportunity, are the result of our activities in other lives. The born musician is a man who has studied music in a previous life, perhaps in several lives, and has therefore built that faculty into his soul. He is a talented musician to-day because he is reaping what he sowed yesterday. It may even be that in previous lives, circumstances, despite all he could do, were too strongly adverse to permit of his actually studying music; but in that case he must have had a steady, continuous *desire* to do so, and persistent desire has brought its fulfillment at last.

Child prodigies are always souls who have acquired their proficiency in a previous life; and it is noticeable how often such children are born into circumstances favorable for their talent. The child violinist often has a father with musical tastes who puts a fiddle into his hand at the earliest possible moment. The gifted child actress appears in a theatrical family, or is born right on the doorstep of Hollywood.

An understanding of Reincarnation not only solves most of life's riddles but serves as a sign-post for all sorts of questions of policy. It constantly furnishes us with guidance for the conduct of social and political life. As for one's private life, it utterly changes the perspective of the whole thing. It is the sovereign remedy for depression and discouragement and regret. It is the gospel of freedom and hope. It makes us realize that there is no mistake that cannot be repaired, that it is never too late, and that no good thing is out of reach of intelligence and work and prayer. It shows us all a future in which there is no limit to the glorious things that we may be and do. A thorough understanding of this doctrine will probably do more than anything else to improve one's character. For instance, it inevitably makes us more tolerant. We cannot but be more merciful toward other people when they displease us if we realize that very largely they are working out personal difficulties that they made in the long ago. We can realize too that no man can act "out of character," and, as misconduct or a bad disposition inevitably brings its own punishment, there is no real reason to be annoyed. When people act badly toward us, we usually think that we know better, and now we shall realize that if this is so we must not retaliate in kind. Someone said, "When a dog bites you, you do not bite the dog to get even," and there is a great moral lesson in this. See the Presence of God in the delinquent, and forget him. Of course, this does not mean that we shall allow him to impose upon us in any way, but we shall no longer be tempted to regard him with resentment.

In general, an understanding of Reincarnation will lead us to do everything we possibly can to make the path of others easier so as to facilitate their personal evolution and that of the race. In our own lives we shall make the most of whatever talents we possess without either sighing for the impossible or fleeing from the inevitable. We shall face up to our difficulties courageously, knowing that there is no problem without a solution and that to run away is to postpone the day of reckoning.

In politics, the implications of Reincarnation are unmistakable. The best political system is the system that will give the greatest personal freedom to the individual. Each one of us must be free to work out his destiny with as little hindrance as possible from outside. Each must have every possible opportunity to exercise the qualities of initiative, self-reliance, resourcefulness, and courage. And these qualities can only be developed where the individual is free. Each must have the chance to make mistakes—and to learn from them. Each must be able to reap the fruit of his own efforts; and those who for one reason or another will not make an effort, must realize that they have to forego the fruit. No political system should put a premium upon idleness, or inefficiency, or stupidity. All the incentives should be in the direction of encouraging intelligence and industry.

The State, of course, should be conceived as existing for the benefit and protection of the individual; never should it be supposed that the individual exists for the sake of the State. On the whole, we may say that the less a government interferes in the life of the private citizen, the better will it be for all concerned. Under the compulsion of force, the individual may actually behave very correctly, because he is obliged to, but because this behavior does not arise from his own desire and initiative, it makes no permanent improvement in his character, and therefore he does not evolve.

Just as all the events of your present life are recorded in the nearer strata of the subconscious mind, so all the events of your past incarnations are recorded in much deeper strata below that. These, however, are not accessible except in very exceptional circumstances for reasons already given. Nevertheless, they are there and help to make you what you are today.

Reincarnation insures your getting all kinds of experience by playing all kinds of roles in the great human drama. And for this reason souls usually change their nationality each time they incarnate because the different nations afford different opportunities for development. The Latin race affords certain opportunities not to be found in the Teutonic race, for example, and the Teutonic race furnishes conditions that are not to be found among Latins. In the same way, the old world of Europe presents an environment not found in the new countries, and in the New World we have opportunities, and also, of course, problems, that the people in Europe are not required to meet. We have already seen that the circumstances into which a soul is born are the natural results of his previous conduct, but this is only another way of saying that these circumstances will supply just the material he needs for further development if he will take advantage of them.

Here it may be well to issue a word of warning. There are people who make fools of themselves about

Reincarnation. This is only to be expected because every great universal truth is sure to be misunderstood or misapplied by some people. A fool will wrest any piece of knowledge to his own confusion, no matter what it is. All the great truths of religion and philosophy have been caricatured by immature minds from time to time, and so we sometimes find obviously undeveloped souls claiming to be reincarnations of some of the most distinguished figures in history. I suppose we have all met the feebleminded individual who was Shakespeare or Napoleon in his less developed days. And self-styled reincarnations of Cleopatra and Joan of Arc adorn many small tea parties up and down the country today, and bore people with their foolish talk. Of course, all this means nothing except that foolish people are finding one more opportunity to be foolish. People who really can remember previous lives are excessively reticent concerning any reference to them. Reincarnation is true and none the less so because it is sometimes misunderstood.

As you think over the truth of Reincarnation and gradually assimilate it—for an adequate realization of what this great truth really means is not to be obtained in a day or two—you will be astonished at the number of otherwise insoluble problems which it clears up. The major problems of life are logically and satisfactorily explained by Reincarnation, and all sorts of minor difficulties which have puzzled you from time to time fall easily into place too when the great scheme of things is understood.

Consider the problem of the rise and fall of nations, for example. All through history nations and empires have risen into prominence and power, have flourished for a time, and then gradually decayed. But why should this be the case? Historians have described the process, but the reasons for it have completely baffled them. The Roman Empire is an excellent example. Why did the Roman Empire "decline and fall"? Orthodox historians have not the faintest notion. They describe the fact but cannot explain it. The Goths and Vandals were able to destroy it—but why? And why not several generations sooner or later? Nobody who does not understand Reincarnation knows. Various reasons for the fall of Rome which were put forward in the past are seen today to be absurd (some people in the Middle Ages were convinced that the fall of Rome was due to the unnatural Roman habit of constantly bathing, especially in hot water!) and the experts remain baffled.

The fashion today is to make economic conditions responsible for everything, but this is to confuse cause with effect, to put the cart before the horse, because economic conditions do not produce man's mentality; it is the human mentality that produces the economic environment. *The materialist conception of history** is one more superstition on its way to the ash-can. (The Indians lived in the same material environment that we do, but our conditions of life are entirely different from theirs because our mentalities are entirely different.) The real cause for both the rise and fall of Rome, was this: For several hundred years advanced and capable souls reincarnated in the Roman nation because that group provided the best opportunity for their further development, and for the development of the race. Being the kind of people they were, they built up and organized that great world state, doing a work for humanity second to none in importance, and making great progress themselves. Then, having worked

*Karl Marx.

out this phase, they passed on to other activities, and an inferior grade of souls incarnated in the Roman nation, and she gradually declined. That is the true and simple explanation.

Many of us have ourselves seen a similar process at work on a small scale. An able and energetic man spends his life building up a successful business. Then, his work done, he passes on, and he is succeeded by his son, or someone else, a person of mediocre talents or weak character, and at once the business begins to go downhill, ending finally in the bankruptcy court. One often sees the same process in connection with a social or political club or other organization. It is formed and made successful by a few capable individuals, and then for one reason or another they gradually drop out, and, being succeeded by inferior people, the enterprise gradually fails.

This, again, is the explanation of the decay of classical Greece. "The glory that was Greece" preceded "the grandeur that was Rome" into oblivion because the glorious souls who made Greece glorious went onward, and were followed by much younger and less developed souls. Of course this was really no tragedy. There would be no point racially or individually in those Greeks going on doing the same things over and over again. They passed on to learn new and different lessons, and their successors obtained an opportunity to take, what was for them, the next step. For example, Praxiteles having learned so well the lesson of artistic expression, may have reappeared hundreds of years later to learn the lessons inherent in the life of a farmer or a sailor or a merchant.

Just as like *attracts* like, so like *produces* like. This is what is called a Cosmic Law, which means that it is universally true throughout the whole of existence, not only throughout the entire physical universe, but right up through the higher planes to the Heart of God Himself. Always, like produces like. As Jesus put it, you do not gather grapes from thorns or figs from this-tles; and he also said, *by their fruits ye shall know them.** So it is with our thoughts and words and deeds. As we sow, we reap. When we sow good, we reap good, and when we sow evil, we reap trouble and suffering. When we sow a little good, we reap a little good; and when we sow a great deal of good, we reap a great deal of good. When we sow a little evil, we reap a little suf-fering; and when we sow a great deal of evil, we reap a great deal of suffering. This is the great Law of Cause and Effect, and it is amazing that people seem to un-derstand it as little as they do. No one expects to sow one plant in the ground and reap another. No one ex-pects to mix copper and tin together and get steel. No one expects to put apples and dough in the oven and get out pumpkin pie; but in the less tangible region of deeds and events, almost everyone seems to think at times that he really can sow one thing and reap an-other. Yet the truth is that as we sow, so shall we reap, sometimes almost immediately, sometimes after a long, long interval; but always, sooner or later, *like pro-duces like.*

In the East this law of cause and effect is known as Karma and the term is a convenient one. But whatever we choose to call it, the law of nature still stands, that as we sow, we shall reap. As we have seen, the condi-tions into which you were born in this life are the out-come of the way in which you have lived in previous lives, and your circumstances today are the outcome of your life up to the present. It naturally follows there-

*Read Matthew 7:15–20; Luke 6:43–45.

fore that you can be happy and well in the future if you will begin now to try to live up to the highest that you know, and take every opportunity to help and serve others in any way that may be open to you.

No matter what mistakes you have made in the past or what opportunities you have wasted, you can overtake them all now; for your future stretches out to infinity and it is never too late with God. If you have a bad conscience about something, no matter how much evil you have sown, you can be free. Cease the wrong conduct, make whatever reparation, if any, is possible, make your peace with God, and then turn your back on the past and never think about it again. Remember that to harbor useless regrets is remorse instead of repentance, and remorse is a sin.

Note very carefully that Karma is not punishment. If you touch a red hot stove, you will burn your finger. This will hurt you, and perhaps incapacitate you for a few days, but it is not punishment, only a natural consequence. Nevertheless it is a benign and reformative thing, for after one or two such experiences in childhood, you learn to keep your fingers away from hot iron. If that stove did not hurt you, you would some day have your whole hand burned off before discovering your loss. So it is with all natural retribution—you suffer because you have a lesson to learn, but when the lesson is learned, the ill consequences cease, for nature is never vindictive.

Karma, you will now see, so far from being a punishment, is really the perfect opportunity that ever-kindly nature gives us to acquire just the knowledge and experience that we need. Human beings punish one another, grown-ups punish children, and society punishes criminals; but, though we seldom suspect it, these punishments are inflicted chiefly from a desire for revenge, "to get even" with the culprit for the annoyance he has caused, even though we rationalize it in various ways. Nature never punishes, she teaches.

It is unfortunate that some people talk so much about "bad Karma." To begin with, you have seen now that no Karma is bad at all, and, further, such people are dwelling exclusively on the suffering that follows wrong conduct, and ignoring the happiness that follows upon good conduct. It is just as much the Law of Karma that every good and kind and wise thing you have ever said or done has brought you fruit of its own kind and will continue to do so. Especially every moment in your life that you have spent in prayer or meditation will continue to bless and enrich you to the end of time. Here I wish to make it as clear as I possibly can that there is nothing fatalistic about the Law of Karma. You have free will—not omnipotence, but always a choice within reasonable limits—and always you can choose the higher or the lower.

The Law of Karma teaches that by making the best use of whatever talents or advantages we have, even though they be small, we shall win still greater talents and opportunities.* On the other hand, if we neglect to make the best use of our talents and opportunities, we shall lose even what we have. The healthy man who neglects his health will lose it. The man with a musical gift who never practises his music will find someday that his gift has atrophied. The rich man who hoards up his money or spends it all selfishly on himself, instead of using it to do good to others, will either lose his money in this life or else will be born

*Jesus teaches this in Matthew 25:15–30.

into poverty next time. God gave him that talent and he "buries it in a napkin."

Most of the trouble in our lives is not caused by Karma at all but by lack of wisdom in the present. The conditions in which you began your life were karmic, but your everyday experience is made by yourself as you go along. It is a common failing for people to behave unwisely, and then grumble at their difficulties and lay the blame on Karma. "I must have been a dreadful sinner in my last life," a person will say, "my conditions are so miserable now." And yet nine times out of ten, his miseries have nothing to do with Karma but are caused solely by poor judgment now. I knew a student of this subject who constantly talked in this way. He was the proprietor of a small business which was steadily failing, and he was surrounded by debts and other embarrassments. He was full of self-pity and he would enlarge upon his worries, and say what a terrible sinner he must have been in his last life to be "punished" in this way. Now the fact was, as some of his friends well knew, that he had no idea of running a business properly. His shop looked neglected, and the quality of his goods was inferior to that obtainable elsewhere at the same price. He was constantly out of stock of the commonest things that customers would ask for, and he was constantly borrowing money at high interests to overtake other debts. Obviously, all this had nothing to do with Karma. His Karma, as far as it went, was good, because it had given him a business of his own in which many men would have made a great success. His trouble was poor judgment and, to some extent, laziness. Two or three of his friends who realized these facts and grew tired of his complaints, once made an effort to bring the truth home to him for his own good, but their efforts were not well received, and he could not or would not face the truth.

Success in your present life calls for good judgment, industry, and the knowledge that you are really the expression of the Living God; and no stable success can be achieved without these things.

Finally, and perhaps this is the most important point of all, you do not have to accept any set of conditions or any kind of Karma if you will rise *above* it in consciousness. Any difficulty, any dilemma, can be surmounted by whole-hearted prayer. A given difficulty can only confront you on its own level. Rise above that level through prayer and meditation and the difficulty will melt away. You do not, as so many people think, have to sit down and eat your Karma with as good grace as possible, if you can rise above that situation in consciousness. On its own level you have to accept it—you cannot transmute it *there*. But rise above any ordeal in consciousness and you will be free from it—for the Christ is Lord of Karma.*

> Our birth is but a sleep and a forgetting
>   The Soul that rises with us, our Life's Star,
>   Hath had elsewhere its setting,
>   And cometh from afar;
>   Not in entire forgetfulness,
>   And not in utter nakedness,
>   But trailing clouds of glory do we come
>   From God, who is our home.
>   —Wordsworth

*See *The Sermon on the Mount,* Chapter Six; and *What Is Scientific Prayer?* (page 259).

Sowing and Reaping

Whatsoever a man soweth that shall he also reap.

T HERE is no such thing as luck. Nothing ever happens by chance. Everything, good or bad, that comes into your life is there as the result of unvarying, inescapable Law. And the only operator of that law is none other than *yourself*. No one else has ever done you any harm of any kind, or ever could do so, however much it may seem that he did. Consciously or unconsciously you have yourself at some time or other produced every condition desirable or undesirable that you find in either your bodily health or your circumstances today. You, and you alone, ordered those goods; and now they are being delivered. And as long as you go on thinking wrongly about yourself and about life, the same sort of difficulties will continue to harass you. For every seed must inevitably bring forth after its own kind, and *thought is the seed of destiny*.

Yet there is a simple way out of trouble. Learn how to think rightly instead of wrongly, and conditions at once begin to improve until, sooner or later, all ill-health, poverty, and inharmony must disappear. Such is the Law. Life need not be a battle; it can, and should be a glorious mystical adventure; but living is a science.

This is one way of stating the Great Law. Read and reread it at regular intervals, and it will inevitably change your outlook on life.

What Is Scientific Prayer?

S CIENTIFIC prayer or spiritual treatment is really the lifting of your consciousness above the level where you have met your problem. If only you can rise high enough in thought, the problem will then solve itself. That is really the only problem you have—to rise in consciousness. The more "difficult," which means the more deeply rooted in your thought, is the problem concerned, the higher you will have to rise. What is called a small trouble, will yield to a slight rise in consciousness. What is called serious difficulty, will require a relatively higher rise. What is called a terrible danger or hopeless problem, will require a considerable rise in consciousness to overcome it—but that is the only difference.

Do not waste time trying to straighten out your own or other people's problems by manipulating thought —that gets you nowhere—but raise your consciousness, and the action of God will do the rest.

Jesus healed sick people and reformed many sinners by raising his consciousness above the picture they presented. He controlled the winds and the waves in the same way. He raised the dead because he was able to get as high in consciousness as is necessary to do this.

To raise your consciousness you must positively withdraw your attention from the picture for the time being (*The Golden Key*), and then concentrate gently upon spiritual Truth. You may do this by reading the Bible or any spiritual book that appeals to you, by going over any hymn or poem that helps you in this way, or by the use of one or more affirmations, just as you like.

I know many people who have secured the necessary elevation of consciousness by browsing at random through the Bible. A man I know was saved in a terrible shipwreck by quietly reading the Ninety-first Psalm. Another man healed himself of a supposedly hopeless disease by working on the one affirmation, "God is Love," until he was able to realize something of what that greatest of all statements must really mean.

If you work with affirmations, be careful not to get tense; but there is no reason why you should not employ all these methods in turn, and also any others that you can think of. Sometimes a talk with a spiritual person gives you just the lift that you need. It matters not how you rise so long as you do rise.

"I bare you on eagles' wings, and brought you unto Myself."

The Presence

G OD is the only Presence and the only Power. God is fully present here with me, now. God is the *only* real Presence—all the rest is but shadow. God is perfect Good, and God is the cause only of perfect Good. God never sends sickness, trouble, accident, temptation, nor death itself; nor does He authorize these things. We bring them upon ourselves by our own wrong thinking. God, Good, can cause only good. The same fountain cannot send forth both sweet and bitter water.

I am Divine Spirit. I am the child of God. In God I live and move and have my being; so I have no fear. I am surrounded by the Peace of God and all is well. I am not afraid of people; I am not afraid of things; I am not afraid of circumstances; I am not afraid of myself; for God is with me. The Peace of God fills my soul, and I have no fear. I dwell in the Presence of God, and no fear can touch me. I am not afraid of the past; I am not afraid of the present. I am not afraid for the future; for God is with me. The Eternal God is my dwelling place and underneath are the everlasting arms. Nothing can ever touch me but the direct action of God Himself, and God is Love.

God is Life; I understand that and I express it. God is Truth; I understand that and I express it. God is Divine Love; I understand that and I express it. I send out thoughts of love and peace and healing to the whole universe: to all trees and plants and growing things, to all beasts and birds and fishes, and to every man, woman and child on earth, without any distinction. If anyone has ever injured me or done me any kind of harm, I fully and freely forgive him now, and the thing is done with forever. I loose him and let him go. I am free and he is free. If there is any burden of resentment in me I cast it upon the Christ within, and I go free.

God is Infinite Wisdom, and that Wisdom is mine. That Wisdom leads and guides me; so I shall not make mistakes. Christ in me is a lamp unto my feet. God is Infinite Life, and that Life is my supply; so I shall want for nothing. God created me and He sustains me. Divine Love has foreseen everything, and provided for everything. One Mind, One Power, One Principle. One God, One Law, One Element. Closer is He than breathing, nearer than hands and feet.

I am Divine Spirit, the Child of God, and in the Presence of God I dwell forever. I thank God for Perfect Harmony.

The Word of Power

PRAY regularly for the ability to pray in the right way: I am Divine Spirit. In God I live, and move, and have my being. I am part of the self-expression of God, and I therefore express perfect harmony. I individualize Omniscience. I have direct knowledge of Truth. I have perfect intuition. I have spiritual perception. I know. God is my Wisdom; so I cannot err. God is my Intelligence; so I am always thinking rightly. There is no waste of time, for God is the only Doer. God works through me; so I am always working rightly, and there is no danger of my praying wrongly. I think the right thing, in the right way, at the right time. My work is always well done, for my work is God's work. The Holy Spirit is continually inspiring me. My thoughts are fresh, and new, and clear, and powerful with the might of Omnipotence. My prayers are the handiwork of the Holy Ghost—powerful as the eagle and gentle as the dove. They go forth in the name of God Himself, and they cannot return unto me void. They shall accomplish that which I please, and prosper in the thing whereto I send them. I thank God for this.

The Holy Ghost, whom the Father will send in my name, shall teach you all things.—John 14:26.

And whatsoever ye shall ask in my name, that will I do.
—John 14:13.

If ye abide in me, and my words abide in you, ye shall ask what ye will, and it shall be done unto you.—John 15:7.

Ask, and ye shall receive, that your joy may be full.
—John 16.24.

Blessing and Cursing

L IFE is a reflex of mental states. As far as *you* are concerned, the character that things will bear will be the character that you first impress upon them. *Bless a thing and it will bless you. Curse it and it will curse you.* If you put your condemnation upon anything in life, it will hit back at you and hurt you. If you bless any situation, it has no power to hurt you, and even if it is troublesome for a time it will gradually fade out—if you sincerely bless it.

We are told, you remember, that whatever name Adam gave to an animal—that was its name; and of course you know that the name of a thing means its character. Adam said to one animal, "You are a tiger, ferocious," and so it was. To another, he said, "You are a gazelle, gentle and kind," and so it was. Now, Adam is Everyman, and until we learn to give good names, to "christen" everything, we shall have enemies of various kinds to deal with.

Bless your body. If there is anything wrong with a particular organ, bless that organ. (Of course, you must bless the organ and not the disease.) Bless your home. Bless your business. Bless your associates. Turn any seeming enemies into friends by blessing them. Bless the climate. Bless the town, and the state, and the country.

Bless a thing and it will bless you.

So shall my word be that goeth forth out of my mouth: it shall not return unto me void, but it shall accomplish that which I please, and it shall prosper in the thing whereto I sent it. —Isaiah 55:11.

But we speak the wisdom of God in a mystery, even the hidden wisdom, which God ordained before the world unto our glory. —I Corinthians 2:7.

Be not afraid nor dismayed by reason of this great multitude; for the battle is not yours, but God's. . . . Ye shall not need to fight this battle: set yourselves, stand ye still, and see the salvation of the Lord with you, O Judah and Jerusalem: fear not, nor be dismayed; to morrow go out against them: for the Lord will be with you. —II Chronicles 20:15, 17.

Let the wicked forsake his way, and the unrighteous man his thoughts: and let him return unto the Lord, and he will have mercy upon him; and to our God, for he will abundantly pardon. —Isaiah 55:7.

The Golden Gate

God is love, and he that dwelleth in love dwelleth in God and God in him.

LOVE is by far the most important thing of all. It is the Golden Gate of Paradise. Pray for the understanding of love, and meditate upon it daily. It casts out fear. It is the fulfilling of the Law. It covers a multitude of sins. Love is absolutely invincible.

There is no difficulty that enough love will not conquer; no disease that enough love will not heal; no door that enough love will not open; no gulf that enough love will not bridge; no wall that enough love will not throw down; no sin that enough love will not redeem.

It makes no difference how deeply seated may be the trouble, how hopeless the outlook, how muddled the tangle, how great the mistake; a sufficient realization of love will dissolve it all. If only you could love enough you would be the happiest and most powerful being in the world.

The two keys of Hell are condemnation and resentment. These can be destroyed permanently by such a treatment as the above.

JESUS SAID: *A new commandment I give unto you, That ye love one another; as I have loved you. . . . By this shall all men know that ye are my disciples, if ye have love one to another.*—John 13:34, 35.

God is love; and he that dwelleth in love dwelleth in God, and God in him.—I John 4:16.

There is no fear in love; but perfect love casteth out fear: because fear hath torment. He that feareth is not made perfect in love.—I John 4:18.

Beloved, let us love one another: for love is of God; and every one that loveth is born of God, and knoweth God. He that loveth not knoweth not God; for God is love.—I John 4:17.

For this is the message that ye heard from the beginning, that we should love one another.—I John 3:11.

We love him, because he first loved us.—I John 4:19

Treatment for
Divine Love

MY soul is filled with Divine Love. I am surrounded by Divine Love. I radiate Love and Peace to the whole world. I have conscious Divine Love. God is Love, and there is nothing in existence but God and His Self-expression. All men are expressions of Divine Love; therefore, I can meet with nothing but the expressions of Divine Love. Nothing ever takes place but the Self-expressing of Divine Love.

All this is true now. This is the actual case, the actual state of affairs. I do not have to try to bring this about, but I observe it already in being now. Divine Love is the actual nature of Being. There is only Divine Love, and I know this.

I perfectly understand what Divine Love is. I have conscious realization of Divine Love. The Love of God burns in me for all humanity. I am a lamp of God, radiating Divine Love to all whom I meet, to all whom I think of.

I forgive everything that can possibly need forgiveness—positively everything. Divine Love fills my heart, and all is well. I now radiate Love to the whole universe, excluding no one. I experience Divine Love. I demonstrate Divine Love.

I thank God for this.

God in Business

A LARGE proportion of what are called business problems really consist in negotiating with other people. All salesmanship, of course, is negotiation between the seller and the purchaser. And successful salesmanship means bringing that negotiation to a termination satisfactory to both parties.

Whether you are seeking a position for yourself or engaging someone else to work for you, the ultimate outcome will depend upon negotiation. You want to find the right person to fill your vacancy or you wish to be engaged for a certain position that you think would suit your requirements very well, and in either case the outcome is a matter of negotiation. Disputes and misunderstandings often arise between two business firms or between a firm and a customer, and here again harmonious relations in the future—which means more business—will depend upon how the present negotiations are conducted.

In fact, every relation in life will be found to depend upon the ability to make harmonious personal adjustments, which is negotiation. In such matters as family and personal disputes, as well as in those things more usually considered under the head of business, the same principle will be found to apply with even greater force if possible.

Now, the secret of successful negotiation can be put into a nutshell. It is this—*See God on both sides of the table*. Claim that God is working through both of you, through yourself and through the person with whom you are dealing. Do not seek by will power to get your own way, but affirm that God's will in that particular matter is being done. Remember that your own way may not be at all good for you. The very thing that you want today may turn out next week to be a nuisance or even a misfortune. Do not try to overreach the other man, to persuade him against his will, or to take the slightest advantage of him in any way. But state your case honestly to the best of your ability; do only what you think is right; and know that God is living and working in your life. Then if you do not make that sale, you will make a better one instead. If you do not get that job, you will get a better one. If you do not make the arrangement that you sought today, a better one will present itself tomorrow.

Never allow yourself to be strained or tense or over-eager. God never hurries; He works without effort. In dealing with fellow man *put God on both sides of the table*, and the outcome will be true success for both parties.

Fifteen Points

I AM REALLY ON THE PATH:

I F I always look for the best in each person, situation, and thing.

If I resolutely turn my back on the past, good or bad, and live only in the present and future.

If I forgive everybody without exception, no matter what he may have done; and if I then forgive MYSELF whole-heartedly.

If I regard my job as sacred and do my day's work to the very best of my ability (whether I like it or not).

If I take every means to demonstrate a healthy body and harmonious surroundings for myself.

If I endeavor to make my life of as much service to others as possible, without interfering or fussing.

If I take every opportunity wisely to spread the knowledge of Truth to others.

If I rigidly refrain from personal criticism, and neither speak nor listen to gossip.

If I devote at least a quarter of an hour a day to prayer and meditation.

If I read at least seven verses of the Bible every day.

If I specifically claim spiritual understanding for myself every day.

If I train myself to give the first thought on waking to God.

If I speak the Word for the whole world every day, say, at noon.

If I PRACTISE the Golden Rule of Jesus instead of merely admiring it. He said, "Whatsoever ye would that men should do to you, do ye even so to them." The important point about the Golden Rule is that I am to practise it whether the other fellow does so or not.

If above all, I understand that whatever I see is but a picture which can be changed for the better by Scientific Prayer.

If you want to demonstrate, ask yourself once a week how far you are observing these points in your life.